RESTRUCTURING OF LIBRARY AND INFORMATION SCIENCE CURRICULUM

CONCEPTS IN COMMUNICATION
INFORMATICS & LIBRARIANSHIP
(CICIL)

For a list of titles in this series,
please see pp. 185-88 at the end of the book

THE AUTHOR

Dr. A. Tejomurty (*b.* 1941) had his post-graduation in Economics. He served in the Madhya Pradesh Government Collegiate Education Department as a lecturer in Economics for about two and-a-half years. He did his Ph.D. in Economics from Vikram University. Turning to Library and Information Science, he did his B.Lib.Sc. from Sagar University, and M.Lib. Inf. Sc. from Vikram University. He did his Ph.D. in Library Science and Documentation from the University of Rajasthan. He is presently Reader and Head in the School of Studies in Library and Information Science, Vikram University, Ujjain.

His teaching tenure bears testimony to his continuous professional interest and writings. He has to his credit ten books, forty-eight papers, and book reviews. He is an active participant in professional seminars. His teaching and writing activities stand prominently on an academic career of first divisions and merit positions.

Dr. A. Tejomurty is a life member of ILA and IATLIS. Presently he is the Secretary of IATLIS.

Concepts in Communication
Informatics & Librarianship-54

General Editor: **S.P. Agrawal**

RESTRUCTURING OF LIBRARY AND INFORMATION SCIENCE CURRICULUM

Edited by
A. TEJOMURTY
Reader and Head
School of Studies in Library and Information Science
Vikram University
Ujjain

CONCEPT PUBLISHING COMPANY, NEW DELHI-110059

AN IATLIS PUBLICATION

ISBN 81-7022-499-3

First Published 1994

Printed and Published by
Ashok Kumar Mittal
A/15-16, Commercial Block, Mohan Garden
NEW DELHI-110059 (India)

Lasertypeset by
Printing Express
H-13, Bali Nagar
NEW DELHI-110015

GENERAL EDITOR'S INTRODUCTION

If one were to look back at the education and training imparted to persons intending to serve in a library set-up, in the early decades of the present century, one would be struck by the metamorphosis they have undergone.

This is not surprising in view of the pace of accretion to human knowledge. In order not to fall out of step with the progress in the developed world, it becomes imperative for us to keep a tab on the scope and content of library and information science and undertake suitable modifications and revisions from time to time.

The present CICIL publication comprising papers prepared for a 1989 seminar has this focus. The kick-off is with the manpower aspect.

While conceding the inevitability of having run of the mill products on our hands, special efforts will have to be made to attract and induce top flight young talent to library profession in the country.

S.P. AGRAWAL

PREFACE

Library and Information Science education in India is at the cross roads. We are facing a challenge, and this must be met boldly and intelligently. The major concern of today is modernization of library operations and services. Computer application to library and information activities is an extremely important area of consideration in this context. Good managers are required to manage the libraries in an intelligent, imaginative, and a responsible manner. Library schools must reorganise courses on library management, keeping in view the changing needs and requirements of libraries.

Restructuring of library and information science curriculum is a major issue of concern today. New technologies, especially information technology, is being introduced today. With this the situation in libraries and information centres is changing. With the advent of new technology, including on-line information system, we have better means of monitoring information use and the ability to make use of it for management of information. Consequently, there is a need for library and information science profession to think and perform differently by exploring new technologies to achieve their mission. Library and information science curriculum needs to be revised drastically to meet the changing requirements. A great responsibility lies with the library schools. Library and information science education in developed countries has started introducing computer and its application in libraries and information centres, and the related courses. UNESCO and other international agencies are providing short-term courses to develop manpower for automation of library and information services, for developing countries too. The curricula of library schools must be revised to include greater amount of information technology.

Today we are witnessing a haphazard growth of library schools in India. We do not need more library schools, but better library schools having adequate resources, aiming at educational excellence and capable of serving as pace setters. We are also observing the establishment of open universities in the recent years, which have started library science courses admitting large number of candidates. This is indeed a serious matter.

A national seminar on "Restructuring of Library and Information Science Curriculum" was held in Rajkot, Gujarat during 14-16 December, 1989. The Seminar was inaugurated by the vice-chancellor, Saurashtra University, Rajkot. The articles published in this volume were presented during the said seminar. My thanks are due to the various authors who have given their permission to include their papers in this volume. I am indebted to Dr. Ganesh Bhattacharya, Professor, DRTC, Bangalore, who worked as Director of the seminar, and to Sri M.P. Satija, who worked as Rapporteur General. My grateful thanks are to M/s Concept Publishing Company, New Delhi, for giving this book form to the manuscript.

DR. A. TEJOMURTY

CONTENTS

LIST OF CONTRIBUTORS

Agrawal, S.S.
Professor and Head
School of Studies in Library and Information Science
Vikram University
Ujjain-456010 (Madhya Pradesh)

Baradol, A.K.
Reader and Chairman
Department of Library and Information Science
Mangalore University
Mangalagangotri-574199 (Karnataka)

Barua, P.
Professor and Head
Department of Library and Information Science
University of Burdwan
Burdwan-713104 (West Bengal)

Bhattacharya, Ganesh
Professor and Head
Documentation Research Training Centre
Bangalore-560059 (Karnataka)

Chatterjee, S.K.
Lecturer
Department of Library and Information Science
University of Burdwan
Burdwan-713104 (West Bengal)

Jagtar Singh
Lecturer
Department of Library and Information Science
Punjabi University
Patiala-147003 (Punjab)

Jena, Pushpanjali
Lecturer
Department of Library and Information Science
Utkal University
Bhubaneswar-751004 (Orissa)

Karisiddappa, C.R.
Reader
Department of Library and Information Science
Karnataka University
Dharwad-580003 (Karnataka)

Kumar, P.S.G.
Reader and Head
Department of Library and Information Science
Nagpur University
Nagpur-440010 (Maharashtra)

Laxman Rao, N.
Reader
Department of Library and Information Science
Osmania University
Hyderabad-500008 (Andhra Pradesh)

Majumdar, K.J.
Reader and Head
Department of Library and Information Science
The M.S. University
Baroda (Gujarat)

Navalani, K. (Miss)
Professor and Head
Department of Library and Information Science
Punjabi University
Patiala-147003 (Punjab)

Sangam, S.L.
Reader
Department of Library and Information Science
Karnataka University
Dharwad-580003 (Karnataka)

Sewa Singh
Reader and Head
Department of Library and Information Science
Gurunanak Dev University
Amritsar-143005 (Punjab)

Shukla, K.H.
Lecturer
Department of Library and Information Science
Gujarat University
Ahmedabad-380009 (Gujarat)

Sivareddy, K.
Professor and Head
Department of Library and Information Science
Andhra University
Visakhapatnam-530003 (Andhra Pradesh)

Sudhir Kumar
Reader
School of Studies in Library and Information Science
Vikram University
Ujjain-456010 (Madhya Pradesh)

Tejomurty, A.
Reader and Head
School of Studies in Library and Information Science
Vikram University
Ujjain-456010 (Madhya Pradesh)

Vaishnava, A.A. (Mrs.)
Lecturer
Department of Library and Information Science
Marathwada University
Aurangabad-431004 (Maharashtra)

Varalakshmi, R.S.R. (Mrs.)
Reader
Department of Library and Information Science
Andhra University
Visakhapatnam-530003 (Andhra Pradesh)

1

STRUCTURAL PLANNING FOR THE DEVELOPMENT OF MANPOWER FOR SECONDARY INFORMATION WORK AND SERVICE

GANESH BHATTACHARYA

1. Introduction

A plan is always the result of a technical operation called "planning". For all practical purposes, the concept of "Planning" is comprehended by the term "Management Activities". These activities include, in general, the following operations relating to any system, organisation, institution, or any component, phase programme, project etc. of any one of those:

(1) Planning, designing and developing,
(2) Organising and staffing,
(3) Operating,
(4) Directing, controlling and co-ordinating,
(5) Maintaining and modernising,
(6) Marketing,
(7) Reporting and evaluating, and
(8) Budgeting.

In fact, all the operations except for item (1) as mentioned earlier, have their respective plans. A general plan, on the other hand refers to all decisions pertaining to each of the operations mentioned above. The purpose of this presentation is to deal with the planning process and the plans pertaining to each of the other operations specially in relation to the "Development of Manpower for Secondary Information Work and

Service"

A few words about the concept of "Manpower" may be regarded as appropriate at this stage. Normally, the term "Manpower" refers to "Power available from or supplied by the physical effort of man". It is also used to refer to "A unit of power assumed to be the rate at which a man performs mechanical work". In this sense, it is generally taken to be "One tenth of a horse power". But, in the context of this presentation, the term "Manpower" has not been used in any one of these senses. On the other hand, the appropriate sense in which it has been used here has been derived from the following generally accepted sense: "The strength (as of a nation, community or industry) expressed in terms of available persons who are competent to be regarded as human resources constituting the strength of a nation for work and service in the different vital spheres of the concerned nation".

If we consider the development of manpower in the sense as mentioned above, we have to recognize a system producing this "Manpower". For the convenience of understanding, the term "Manpower" henceforth should necessarily refer to "Educated Manpower". A system that produces something is normally designated as "Production System". A production system is recognized normally to be man-made system or artificial system. It is not unusual that a production system is normally recognised as a Commodity Production System or Service Production System. But, in fact, it is not always necessary to be so. For, there are man-made production systems which are meant for producing (1) New information; (2) New processes; and (3) New Products. Such systems are called "Research and Development System" (R&D System). Analogously, there are man-made production systems which are meant for developing educated manpower. Such a system may be called an "Educated Manpower Development System" (EMDS). All educational systems are in fact EMDS. Our specific concern for this presentation is an EMDS pertaining to Secondary Information Work and Service. The familiar examples of such an EMDS may be a school, a college, an university or an institution of higher learning.

The distinct mode of thinking that should necessarily be operative in thinking about a system in general, and an EMDS in particular is known as "Systems-Approach", developed on the basis of the "General Systems Theory" formalized by LUDWIG VON BERTALANFY. The "Systems-Approach" serves as the guideline for any sort of planning giving rise to a plan. In dealing with the "Development of Manpower for Secondary Information Work and Service", this presentation has been guided by the "Systems-Approach" to the extent necessary and sufficient.

2. Operational Definition of Systems-Approach

For the sake of convenience, it is necessary at this stage to formulate an operational definition of the concept "Systems-Approach". For all practical purposes, a system is a complex entity deemed to be a whole; and it is made up of structurally and functionally related non-wholes or components. Any such relatively non-whole or component, in turn, may be deemed to be a whole; and which again is found to be made up of structurally and functionally related sub-components. By implication, any system may have its own super-system on the one hand; and its own super-system on the other. In the case of a man-made production system, the concepts of "Environment Goal" have to be taken into consideration. For all such systems function in a specified environment to achieve a well-defined goal.

Work pertaining to a man-made system predominantly involves (1) Systems-Design or Systems-Synthesis; and (2) Systems-Evaluation. Both these operations are based on a basic operation known as Systems Analysis. All these activities call for a strategy known as "System Analysis". Systems-Approach consists of applying a synthetic mode of thought as well as an analytic mode of thought for carrying out all the operations comprehended by the term "Management Activities" as mentioned earlier. In the synthetic mode of thought, a system is viewed as a sub-system or a super-system. In the analytic mode of thoughts, a system is explained in terms of its specific structure functions and other attributes. The term "Structure" refers to the part, i.e. "Components" and their inter-relationship. Neither of two modes of thought negates the value of the other. The understanding of a system that can be gained by one mode of thought, cannot be gained by other. In the process of complete understanding of a system, one mode of thought complements the other.

Operationally, Systems-Approach consists of (1) raising a set of check-questions corresponding to each mode of thought; (2) finding precise answers to each set of questions; and (3) deriving from these answers the necessary guidelines in carrying out the different "Management Activities" as mentioned earlier. For example, corresponding to the synthetic mode of thought, the set of questions generally raised consists of the following:

(i) What constitutes the immediate environment of the system concerned?

(ii) What are all the super-system of different removes of which the system, concerned may be deemed to be a sub-system?

(iii) What is the overall objective (goal) of each of those super-systems of different removes?

(iv) What are all the coordinate systems?

(v) What is the overall objective of each of the coordinate systems, the achievement of which contributes to the achievement of the overall objective of the immediate super-system?

(vi) What is the overall objective of the concerned system?

Analogously, corresponding to the analytic mode of thought, the set of questions generally raised consisted of the following:

(vii) What are all the components of different levels of the concerned system?

(viii) What are all the specific functions of each of these components?

(ix) What are all the other attributes that are essential for each of these components which would contribute to the accomplishment of its specific functions?

(x) What is the level of performance efficiency of each of these components?

This presentation is, to the extent warranted and feasible, based on conscious application of the systems approach as operationally defined in this section.

3. Notions of "Planning" and "Plans"

Before proceeding further, it appears to be necessary to develop a clear conception of the notions "Planning" and "Plans". An attempt has already been made earlier to enumerate the major "Management Activities". A professional who displays great regard for scientific management principles and rules of procedure in carrying out the "Management Activities", as mentioned earlier, is a "Manager" in the technical sense of the term. A 'Manager' has to make sure that every activity is performed to a predesigned scheme. While this function of his means "Control", the pre-designed scheme is his plan. In this explanation, 'Planning" is, indeed, decision-making which relates to the whole gamut of "Hows" of all "Management techniques, determination of which is a pre-requisite to ascertain the correct path." The control of any man-made production system is primarily dependant upon its planning. The significance of planning in general lies in the fact: "The control of production system without planning is a myth. A system is a system because of planning, otherwise, it becomes random in nature. Planning ensures meaningful decisions in place of *ad hoc* choices". In practice, the courses available for carrying out management activities are usually many, at least more than one. This is a situation that admits of alternatives. Fundamentally, planning consists of choosing the most appropriate course from among its all possible alternatives. There are many factors external to a production system that may interfere with the actual operation of the course chosen. In the context of an anticipation of those factors, planning, to a large extent, consists of making things happen that would not otherwise happen. For this purpose, need arises to analyse the objectives and pertinent facts to arrive at considered calculations and conclusions. On the basis of these findings only, conscious decisions are made about the courses. Planning, in general, is thus an intellectual process. A professional in any field has to plan to accomplish his target. This is so even if he is working under strict orders and procedures. In such cases, his area of planning is restricted to his area of work. Planning, in such circumstances, may be considered to be a key to his success. The pervasiveness of planning function, in general, is quite extensive and intensive.

In fact, the work at every level of a production system can be logically divided into three basic functions: (1) Planning; (2) Implementing (Doing); and (3) Inspecting (Controlling). The efficiency and effectiveness of a systems-performance is directly a function of coordination. "Coordination" calls for the establishment of some natural forces to check and maintain balance. The categorization of all systems-tasks into three basic functions, as mentioned earlier, is considered to be the most conducive for the establishment of such natural forces.

It has been mentioned earlier that the foundation of planning rests on decision-making. In this sense, planning turns out to be a selection of the right decisions from among their all possible alternatives. As a result, the products of planning, as a process, are "plans". In this sense, a plan may take the form of things such as the following:

(i) The structural design of system with the specification of functions;
(ii) The statement of objectives;
(iii) The statement of policies and principles;
(iv) The statement of rules of procedure for all operations;
(v) The organizational chart;
(vi) The guidelines for staff selection;
(vii) The guidelines for staff posting;
(viii) The statement of duties and responsibilities of staff members;
(ix) The statement of inspection procedure;
(x) The statement of monitoring procedure;
(xi) The maintenance specifications;
(xii) The guidelines for report generation and statement of reporting instruction;
(xiii) The specification of evaluation procedure and criteria;
(xiv) Budget;
(xv) Program Documents; and
(xvi) Project documents.

The above list includes "Program Documents" and "Project Documents". It may be noted here that such documents may have to incorporate in it all the other items mentioned in the list. For this reason, such documents are treated as "General Plans" for the programs and projects as the case may be. Similarly, a general plan for a system incorporates within it all the items included in the list.

It is necessary to state here that this presentation with all the items listed above in relation to the concerned EMDS. The purpose of this presentation is primarily to focus on the factors to be taken into consideration for developing a comprehensive plan of the EMDS pertaining to secondary information work and service. In the course of achieving this objective, obviously some elements of plans may have to be dealt with in general terms.

4. Implications of Professional Education

The development of manpower for Secondary Information Work and Service has to be ensured through appropriate education and training. Such education and training have to be regarded as "PROFES-

SIONAL" in nature. Any thinking in regard to the development of professional manpower must take into account, at the very outset, all the necessary implications of professional education and training. For, the planning in this regard should necessarily be governed by the implication of professional education and training. For this reason, an attempt is being made here in that direction.

All professions are "Callings". The term "Calling" implies that a person doing a professional work or rendering a professional service enjoys the right of claiming and receiving payments. Unfortunately, all callings are not professions. A calling attains the status of a profession by qualifying itself with the following attributes:

(i) The practice of a profession calls for the utilisation of specialized knowledge and skill;
(ii) To acquire such specialized knowledge and skills, a would-be professional has to undergo long and intensive preparation including learning of skills and methods as well as understanding of the scientific, historical, and scholarly principles underlying such skills and methods;
(iii) A profession maintains by force of organisation or concerted opinion a high standard of achievement and conduct;
(iv) A profession commits its members to continuing education; and
(v) A professional is engaged in work which has for its prime purpose the rendering of a public service.

Besides the attributes mentioned earlier, a profession displays its self-consciousness in the following ways:

(i) Alertness about the inadequacy of available fixed time training and educational programmes for the profession;
(ii) Introduction of theoretical analysis of professional work;
(iii) Attempts to standardize the practice of the profession;
(iv) Concern with low standards, bad workmanship, and indifferent handling of clientele;
(v) Attempts to establish co-ordination and cooperation among the practitioners;
(vi) Protest against the lack of recognition for the profession or occupation; and
(vii) Belief in the emergence of a new and different discipline with the wide applications.

One intending to enter into a profession, cannot be expected to be readily conscious about the implication of "profession". The responsibility of making one conscious about the implications rests with professional education and training one is to undergo. The consideration of this factor seems to play the most important role in formulating the policy pertaining to professional education and training. All other aspects relating to professional education and training flow from this consideration. Education and training for secondary information work and service cannot be an exception to this professional consideration. One of the important objectives of a professional EMDS, therefore, is to help each student develop the necessary consciousness about the implications of professional education and training. There is always an economic consideration associated with the implications of professional education and training. The social recognition of a profession has been experienced to be a function of the balance between the demand (actual and potential) and supply. This fact should necessarily be considered as a warning in implementing any professional education or training programme.

It is only professional consciousness that leads to the recognition of the attributes that are expected of a professional. Studies in this area have succeeded to work out a general framework of these required attributes. The ingredients constituting this framework are as follows:

(i) A distinct mode of thinking about the concerned production system;
(ii) A clear conception of the concerned system, its environment, its super-systems, its co-ordinate systems, its components and their respective structures, functions and other necessary attributes;
(iii) A clear conception of all professional technical concepts, principles and postulates;
(iv) Thorough knowledge of the professional techniques, tools, work and service;
(v) Necessary and sufficient knowledge of the machines and equipment (which are usually the results of advances in technology) that can be used profitably to enhance the productivity of the concerned system in terms of its efficiency and effectiveness together with adequate skills to make use of those for the purpose in hand.

Consideration of this expectation suggests some guidelines in a more or less abstract term, as to the identification of the core contents to be incorporated in a course intended to develop "Professional Manpower". Additionally, it furnishes some hints about the teaching and learning methods to be adopted.

5. Concerned EMDS

Till now, the presentation has been devoted to the consideration of the common factors equally significant in the planning of any EMDS. We may now turn to the specific EMDS pertaining to Secondary Information Work and Service (SIWS). For the convenience of the reference, we shall refer to this specific system by using the abbreviation "EMDS/SIWS".

The overall objective of any EMDS is to develop educated manpower having knowledge and skill necessary and sufficient to prosecute further studies for the purpose of acquiring more knowledge and developing more skills so that this man-power can constitute and enrich the collective educational and intellectual strength and competence for work in the different vital spheres of the life of the concerned nation. Consequently, the overall objectives of any discipline oriented EMDS would be totally in conformity with this objective keeping its purview restricted to the concerned discipline. Therefore, the overall objective of the specific EMDS/SIWS has to be analogously in conformity with the overall objective of the general EMDS keeping its purview restricted to the discipline or disciplines forming the foundation of Secondary Information Work and Service (SIWS). Having taken note of the overall objective of the concerned EMDS/SIWS, let us now turn to its structures and functions.

6. Structures and Functions of EMDS/SIWS

The EMDS/SIWS is meant for developing educated manpower having knowledge and skills necessary and sufficient to prosecute further studies for the purpose of acquiring more knowledge and developing more skills so that this manpower can constitute and enrich the collective educational and intellectual strength and competence for secondary information work and service contributing to the development of the nation in all its vital spheres. To ensure efficient and effective performance of the EMDS/SIWS, it is essential to recognise two distinct types of primary agencies as its major components. These agencies may be designated as follows:

(i) The promoting agencies; and
(ii) The implementing agencies.

The Promoting Agencies

The promoting agencies should include all the professional bodies concerned with secondary information work and services; and the governmental and semi-governmental bodies concerned with the development in various spheres of life of the nation. The universities and other institutions of higher learning may be recognized as the primary implementing agencies. The importance of the role of information in national development suggests that an organisation falling in the category of promoting agencies must have a wing concerned with pertinent information resources and services, and with the development of manpower for secondary information work and service. The institutions falling in the category of implementing agencies should be concerned with a full complement of programmes deemed to be essential for developing manpower for Secondary Information Work and Service (SIWS), in the true sense of the term. The following sections deal with their respective objectives and programmes.

6.1 *Objectives of Promoting Agencies*

The objectives of a promoting agencies may be enumerated as follows:

(i) To determine the contemporary and future professional manpower requirements for information work and service in its fields of interest; and to help the development of an adequate professional manpower of requisite levels to meet the requirements by extending necessary and sufficient financial support to the appropriate implementing agencies;
(ii) To help the development of manpower capable of participating efficiently and effectively in teaching and research projects in information science including library science and documentation specially by extending financial support;
(iii) To help the development of expertise and excellence in the field of information science by supporting pertinent research projects in the appropriate field;

(iv) To initiate and support continuing education projects in the field of information science; and

(v) To help the placement at the right professional of the right place; and to ensure that the service conditions of professionally trained persons engaged in information work and service are on par with those scientific personnel.

Obviously, a promoting agency may have to keep its purview restricted to (i) Receiving project proposals from implementing agencies; (ii) Evaluating such project proposals; and (iii) Extending financial support for implementing the proposals. The actual project work is to be carried out by the implementing agencies.

6.2 *Programmes of Activity of Promoting Agencies*

To achieve the objectives mentioned earlier, the activities of a promoting agency may be organised into the following support-programmes corresponding to its different objectives:

(i) Education Programme;
(ii) Teachers' Training Programme;
(iii) Research Programme;
(iv) Continuing Education Programme; and
(v) Placement Programme.

In addition to those programme, it will be necessary for a promoting agency to initiate a–

(vi) Publication Programme to complement other programmes.

Depending upon the situation, many of the activities under these programmes are to be carried out in collaboration with other promoting agencies having similar objectives. The activities to be carried out under different programmes are enumerated below:

Education Programmes

The activities under the education programmes would be as follows:

(i) To ascertain the professional manpower requirements;
(ii) To ascertain the extent of existing educational and training facilities, and the potential of different institutions to meet the requirements of different levels;

(iii) To identify the inadequacies in regard to levels of education and training faculty members, subject specialization of students, course contents, physical facilities, utilisation of machines and equipment (which are normally the products of advances in technology), and to recommend measures to meet these inadequacies and wherever warranted, to extend financial support for the purpose;

(iv) To recognize expertise and excellence at the level of individuals and institutions, and to extend incentives for their further development;

(v) To help the development of noise-free curricula and course contents (syllabi) for different levels of education, and to recommend their adoption by different institutions;

(vi) To initiate and support resource sharing between and among different institutions including inter-institutional teacher-exchange programmes;

(vii) To help development of criteria for identifying outstanding students; and to extend incentives in the form of stipend, scholarship, etc;

(viii) To initiate and support work-*cum*-education project;

(ix) To help development of criteria for judging the standard of performance of different institutions engaged in the development of manpower for information and services; and

(x) To initiate and support the establishment of a national institute of information sciences.

Teachers' Training Programme

The activities under the teachers' training programme would be as follows:

(i) To initiate and support teachers training programmes;

(ii) To help the development of appropriate methodologies of teaching and learning different topics at different levels of education, and to recommend their adoption by different institutions; and

(iii) To support the acquisition and utilization of machines and equipment, such as, computers and audio-visual aids meant for aiding teaching, learning, and research processes.

Research Programme

The activities under the research programme would be as follows:

(i) To help development of criteria for evaluating project proposals;
(ii) To initiate and support research projects;
(iii) To initiate and support development of national standards and specifications, techniques and tools through research; and
(iv) To recognize expertise and excellence at the levels of individuals and institutions on the basis of objective evaluation of their respective research achievements; and to extend incentives.

Continuing Education Programme

The activities under the continuing education programme would be as follows:

(i) To sponsor conferences, symposia, seminars, workshops, institutes, refresher courses, special lectures, extension lectures etc;
(ii) To offer opportunities to professionals to attend the continuing education programmes and projects; and
(iii) To identify the areas appropriate for refresher courses, and to recommend and support their organisation by competent implementing agencies.

Placement Programme

The activities under the placement programme would be as follows:

(i) To maintain a register of qualified and experienced professionals;
(ii) To establish contact with prospective employers and to maintain a register of their respective requirements;
(iii) To help the placement of the right professional at the right job;
(iv) To help the establishment of degree-equivalence for employment purposes;
(v) To recommend qualifications and experience for different

levels of professional positions together with their respective duties and responsibilities; and

(vi) To recommend salary-scales and service conditions whenever feasible for different levels of professional positions.

Publication Programme

The activities under the publication programme would primarily be to initiate and support publications pertaining to or originating out of different programmes. Usually publication of this type would take forms, such as the following:

(i) Survey reports;
(ii) Course materials, manuals, text books, hand-books etc.;
(iii) Guides for curriculum developments;
(iv) Documents on teaching techniques;
(v) Primary periodicals disseminating research results and similar findings;
(vi) Advance treatises;
(vii) Research and technical reports;
(viii) Standards and specifications;
(ix) Codes for bibliographic description;
(x) Vocabulary control devices such as schemes for classification, thesauri, classauri, etc;
(xi) Manuals for using different systems for subject indexing;
(xii) Proceedings of seminars, conferences, etc.;
(xiii) Secondary periodicals such as indexing periodicals, abstracting periodicals and state-of-the-reports including other products of information analysis and consolidation.

6.2 *Objectives of the Implementing Agencies*

It has been already mentioned earlier that in relation to the development of manpower for secondary information work and service, the implementing agencies would consist of the discipline-oriented departments/division/units etc. of organizations, such as Universities and other Institutions of higher learning. The objectives of an implementing agency may be enumerated as follows:

(i) To develop professional/semi-professional manpower for

secondary information work and service. It may be noted here that the aim of the implementing agency is to help the trainees equip themselves with adequate knowledge and skills to carry out secondary information work and service of different professional levels. This implies that they should be capable of applying scientific method with proper understanding of the principles underlying those methods. Their responsibilities should necessarily include, on the one hand, all technical operations and, on the other, all management activities as mentioned earlier;

(ii) To develop professional manpower capable of participating efficiently and effectively in the teaching and research programmes pertaining to foundation disciplines of secondary information work and service; and

(iii) To contribute to the development of information sciences including library science and documentation by doing, guiding, and supporting research and development in the concerned fields.

6.2.1 *Programme of Activity of Implementing Agencies*

To achieve the objective as mentioned earlier, the activities of an implementing agency may have to be organized into the following programmes:

(i) Education and training programme;
(ii) Research programme;
(iii) Continuing education programme;
(iv) Advisory service programme;
(v) Extension programme;
(vi) Faculty development programme;
(vii) Employment information programme; and
(viii) Publication programme.

The activities under the different programme would be as enumerated below under each of the programmes.

Education and Training Programme

The activities under the education and training programme would be as follows:

(i) To conduct courses leading to various professional and semi-professional degrees, diplomas etc. such as Bachelor's Degree, Master's Degree, Pre-Doctoral Degree, Doctoral Degree for Professionals and Diploma, Certificate etc. for semi-professionals;
(ii) To develop and apply appropriate methodologies of teaching and learning various topics; and
(iii) To keep the curricula and syllabi up-to-date and noise-free from the point of view of meeting the requirements to different environments.

Research Programme

The activities under the research programme would be as follows:

(i) To guide research for partial fulfilment of requirements of courses leading to various professional degrees;
(ii) To guide research leading to pre-doctoral and doctoral degrees;
(iii) To promote, support, carry out and conduct continuing research; and
(iv) To organise regular meetings to help researchers exchange ideas among themselves.

It may be noted here that developing advanced course materials, designing tools, inventing and improving upon techniques; developing models, standards and specifications, guidelines etc. constitute some of the concrete targets of the research programme.

Continuous Education Programme

The activities under the continuing education programme would be as follows:

(i) To organise and conduct conferences, symposia, workshop, institutes, refresher courses , special lectures etc.; and
(ii) To participate activity in Continuing Education Programmes run by other agencies.

Advisory Service Programme

The primary activity under the Advisory Service Programme would be to render advisory and consultative services specially in the design and development of information centres, systems services, professional techniques and professional tools. It may be noted here that the term "Information Centre" refers to organizations such as, Libraries, Documentation Centres, Information Analysis and Consolidation Centres and Data Centres.

Extension Programme

The results of research carried out by an Institution are normally disseminated through professional primary periodicals. However, many of the researches in the field of information science are typically descriptive-oriented. Usually, the organizations dealing with a given discipline, is interested in the results of researches oriented towards the concerned discipline. In such a situation, it becomes imperative for the researchers to demonstrate the usefulness of their research results in an organization dealing with the concerned discipline. The primary activity of their extension programme would be to develop a mechanism for carrying out such demonstration activities in interested organisation.

Faculty Development Programme

The activity under the Faculty Development Programme would be as follows:

(i) To provide opportunity to every individual member of the faculty that would ensure his development, both intellectual and professional. It may be noted here that the active participation by the members of the faculty in all programmes as mentioned earlier would definitely ensure their respective professional advancement; and

(ii) To take advantage of opportunities relating to Faculty Development offered by other organizations, it may be noted here that normally the advantage of such opportunities are taken by providing opportunity to individual members of the faculty to participate actively in the continuing education programme meant specially for professionals and run by other agencies.

Employment Information Programme

The activity under the Employment Information Programme would be as follows:

(i) To establish contact with employing organisations and promoting agencies; and to take note of their requirements relating to professionals by maintaining a file of profiles of such requirements;
(ii) To maintain a register of trained persons seeking employment;
(iii) To maintain a register of job opportunities; and
(iv) To supply information to trained persons about job opportunities.

It may be noted here that it is extremely difficult to assure a trained person an appropriate job opportunity specially in a country like India. But, experience shows that a mechanism of contact between employing organizations and implementing agencies goes a long way in finding jobs for the trained persons.

Publication Programme

The activity under the publication programme would be to publish and to get published monographs, reports, papers, course materials etc., in the field of information science. Such materials are expected to be generated by the different programme of the implementing agencies.

7. **Programme Implementation Policy**

The following policy-elements should guide the implementation of different programme by the implementing agencies.

(i) Co-ordination of existing educational and training facilities;
(ii) Articulation of various educational and training endeavours;
(iii) Assisting development of strong points of existing educational and training facilities; and
(iv) Encouraging public and private institutions for education and training.

The policy-element that should guide the implementing agencies is the spirit of resource-sharing.

8. Conclusion

It is to note that the essential ingredients of the model furnished here are unknown to the profession of Information Scientists. On the contrary, they have been identified and dealt with elaborately on many occasions. But, in the Systems-Approach, in many situations, there remains a scope of experimenting with the relationship between and among the components till the "Optimization" relating to the efficiency and effectiveness of the system is achieved. Of course, it does not imply that indisciplined imagination can replace rational arguments. A system for the development of manpower for Secondary Information Work and Service (SIWS) is a developing entity; and it is definitely amenable to reconsideration. The model suggested in this paper is just a product of one such reconsideration, based on the study of existing systems and ideas of some leading thinkers; and on personal experience.

Discussion on "Planing" cannot be completed without reference to its product which is known as "Plan for this reason, while dealing with the method of "Planning" and with the factors to be considered for "Planning", a model structural and functional plan also has been worked out primarily to demonstrate the "Planning Process." The whole endeavour pertains to the Development of Educational Manpower for Secondary Information Work and Service. In this context, it may be expected that such a plan should have covered all the other aspects of manpower development, as these aspects may be considered to be essential components of the EMDS considered here. These components are:

(i) Courses of different levels;
(ii) Their respective course contents (curricula and syllabi);
(iii) Duration of the courses;
(iv) Entry qualifications for the courses of different levels;
(v) Teaching/Learning techniques;
(vi) Evaluation procedure and techniques;
(vii) Strategies and forms of Continuing Education and training programmes; and
(viii) Display mechanisms of professional behaviour.

Behind all these aspects of professional education and training lies the selection of knowledge and skills required for information work and service at the advanced level. It may be noted here that the scope of this presentation has been kept confined only to structural planning of the EMDS/SIWS. The reason being that the aspects mentioned earlier have been dealt with quite elaborately on many occasions. The aspect covered by this presentation has not yet been discussed in this form as year.

Further, another important point in relation to the development of educated professional manpower for Secondary Information Work and Service is that an EMDS/SIWS has to be viewed as a major component of the total National Development System. The "National Development" is the ultimate goal of any nation. The notion of national development entails a groupwise well-balanced, coordinatedly integrated development in all the vital spheres of the light of the nation. These spheres include Pure Sciences, Engineering, Medicine, Agriculture, Fine-Arts, Literature, Sports and Recreation, Sociology, Culture, Law, etc. Every nation is obliged to establish its own Nation Development System (NDS). Its overall objective is to ensure and promote national development. The efficient and effective functioning of a national Development System calls for the economic utilization of the resources forming input to the system and these include resources such as, manual, mechanical, financial, material and intellectual resources. Intellectual resources of a nation may be viewed as consisting of (i) the intellectual faculty of the people of the nation; and (ii) information. These two manifestations of intellectual resources are intimately related to each other. Intellectuals use information to generate new information, which in turn enriches the store of existing information, and the cycle goes on and on the gamut of activities concerned with information includes: (i) Generation and utilisation of primary information; (ii) communication of primary information; and (iii) Promotion of the utilisation of primary information through Secondary Information Work and Service. Each national development system, to accomplish its goal, establishes general, mission oriented, and discipline-oriented development systems to take care of these activities. Obviously, any such total information system consists of three primary components corresponding to the major information activities, namely, generation, communication and service. By implication, any discipline-oriented major component of the national development system has to be concerned with Secondary Information Work and Service as an essential obligation. For this reason, they have to play the role of a promoting agency in some form or another in relation to their respective discipline-oriented secondary information work and service. This assumption has formed the basis for recognizing such organizations also as Promoting Agencies. This explanation is furnished here for the purpose of avoiding any misunderstanding about this group of Promoting Agency in relation to Secondary Information Work and Service.

9. References

It is customary to append a list of references with a paper of this type. But, there appears to be a great difficulty in working out such a list. For a very large number of documents have been consulted to work out this general framework of the "Plan" in the form of a model by using the intellectual process of "Logical Abstraction". None of those sources has directly dealt with this framework as presented in this paper. But, they have definitely been contributors in stimulating the generation of this line of thinking. The first attempt of working out such a model was made in my paper entitled "Development of Professional Manpower for Infromation Service: A Model". It was published in the *Journal of Library and Information Science*, Vol.4(2) Dec., 1979; pp 127-143". This article listed 37 items as bibliographic references. Later on, a large number of documents have been consulted to improve upon the earlier line of thinking; and to find justification for the model proposed here.

2

LIBRARY AND INFORMATION SCIENCE CURRICULUM : Some Basic Considerations

C.R. KARISIDDAPPA and S.L. SANGAM

1. Introduction

Curriculum is the heart of any educational system. It play a central role in the educational process. A systematic approach to curriculum aims at improved design of learning situations. Planning and designing of the curriculum in advance can enhance educational programme in a constructive way.[1]

Recent advances in scientific, technological, economic, political, social and cultural spheres in the world over have had a considerable impact on the information requirements of different user groups. As a logical consequence, the activities of the information centres and librarians had to be geared to meet the challenges of the different requirements of the varied groups of users. Therefore, it is imperative that the trained information officer be of a high calibre in academic and professional qualifications and in personal capabilities. Further, it demands that the educational programme offered at various levels by the different schools of library and information science should be based on high and challenging goals and objectives.

Information science, a fast developing field of theory and practice, is becoming increasingly inter-disciplinary. It is a discipline derived from and related to the fields like library science, computer science, communication, behavioural science etc. Therefore, a programme in information studies has to draw upon the expertise in different disciplines. Further, the impact of information technology in information field is now well recognised and therefore the programme should provide adequate practical experience in information technology applications, access to computer facilities with suitable software packages, teaching aids and expertise have to be ensured.

2. Concept of Curriculum

The word curriculum has a latin origin. It means a 'run way' or course which one runs to reach a goal. The Dictionary of education[2] defines curriculum as follows:

(a) a systematic group of courses or sequences of subjects required for graduation or certification in a major field of study;
(b) a general overall plan of the content or specific materials of instruction that the school should offer to the student by way of qualifying him for graduation or certification or for entrance into a professional or vocational field; and
(c) a body of prescribed educative experiences under school supervision, designed to provide an individual with the best possible training and experience to fit him for the society of which he is a part or to qualify him for a trade or a profession.

The analysis of the above mentioned points reveals that the important attributes associated with the concept of curriculum are related to an occupation, objective oriented context, planned learning experiences and criteria for evaluation of student's performance.

2.1 *Difference between Syllabus and Curriculum*

Syllabus is normally a document which lists the subjects, and contents outline with broad time allocations. Functionally a 'syllabus' is generally unidimensional in the sense it merely presents the content or the subject matter to be studied. In the syllabus there is no indication of implementation strategies. But the 'curriculum' is three dimensional because it takes into account the following factors:
(1) the needs of the students; (2) the content; and (3) instructional methodology.

3. Phases of Curriculum Process

The curriculum process, involves four phases:

(i) Design phase;
(ii) Development phase;
(iii) Implementation phase; and
(iv) Evaluation phase.

Viewing from the point of time and operations involved, these phases may be considered as sequential. They are related and interdependent and combine to form a cyclical process, so that the final phase effects the initial one. Each phase is a logical development from the preceding one.

The objectives, major tasks in each phase and the strategies for accomplishing the tasks, are described in the following sections.

3.1 *Curriculum Design Phase*

The main objective of this phase is to determine the general and specific objectivities of particular L&IS course.

(i) For a chosen area of curriculum we have to obtain data on job descriptions and from that prepare the task analysis. These two are often referred to as 'job analysis'. This can be done by a number of methods viz, well designed questionnaires, actual observation of jobs, interview techniques, and judicious combination of all the three mentioned above.

(ii) A detailed analysis of different related jobs will reveal the clusters of knowledge and skills that these jobs demand. These clusters of knowledge and skills are then written in the form of course objectives. These objectives reveal in general and specific terms what the students can do at the end of a specified period of instruction by way of achieving these objectives. The emphasis, as you realize, is one of the specific performances of the students and not on the context itself. While transforming the clusters of knowledge and skills into objectives, the curriculum designer should give consideration to the knowledge and skills that have already been acquired by other words, the curriculum designer must determine:

(a) What abilities the L&IS students possess on entry into the course; and
(b) What abilities the L&IS students will require on leaving the

course. The difference between (a) and (b) is the gap that must be bridged when designing the L&IS curriculum.

3.2 *Curriculum Development Phase*

The Development Phase deals with the development of the instructional resources necessary for achieving the objectives. Tasks to be undertaken in this regard may be listed as follows:

(i) Sequencing the various L&IS subjects;
(ii) Selecting the content in each subject;
(iii) Sequencing the topics in each subject;
(iv) Selecting instructional methods, instructional materials and media in L&IS;
(v) Preparation of plans for instruction (specifically cataloguing and classification practicals);
(vi) Development of tests and other materials needed for evaluation of students' performance;
(vii) Pilot trials of the instructional and evaluation materials prepared;
(viii) Revision of the materials based on the feedback information collected from pilot trials;
(ix) Duplicating or printing and supplying the materials to teachers and students; and
(x) Orienting the teachers in the use of the methods and materials developed for implementation of the new curriculum.

3.3 *Curriculum Implementation Phase*

The third phase in the curriculum process deals with the preparation for and monitoring of the actual implementation of the curriculum. Tasks to be undertaken in this regard are:

(i) Preparation of implementation plans;
(ii) Organising in-service staff development programmes;
(iii) Effecting organisational changes like work distribution, role clarification, provision of support services and streamlining procedures and communication channels;
(iv) Monitoring the implementation process and evaluation of student's performance; and

(v) Collection of feedback information.

The curriculum plan is implemented through the medium of instruction. There are two things to take note i.e. 'intended curriculum' and 'operational curriculum'. Intended curriculum refers to a document containing the objectives of the curriculum, content matter, time schedules, guidelines to teaching and learning programme according to set standards. Whereas the operational curriculum deals with the process of teaching and learning, organization of the class and the milieu in which the instruction takes place. In most of the cases the existing infrastructure in the L&IS schools decides the effective implementation of these curriculum programmes.

There are other factors influencing the effective implementation of curricula which can be classified into the following three groups:

(i) Factors related to the students (aptitude for the subject, proficiency in the language which is used as the medium of instruction, behaviour and motivation;
(ii) Factors related to the teacher (teacher preparedness and teacher's resourcefulness); and
(iii) Factors related to the instructional environment. (Appropriateness of curriculum objectives, adequacy of instructional time, instructional resources, instructional methods and procedures, and task orientation of the class, evaluation procedures and feedback provided to the students).

3.4 *Curriculum Evaluation Phase*

Curriculum evaluation phase is interpreted as the collection and provision of evidence, on the basis of which decisions can be taken about the feasibility, effectiveness, efficiency and educational value of the curricula. It can take place during the time the curriculum is developed for the purpose of guiding the developmental process, or, it takes place after the new curriculum has been implemented for two or three years for the purpose of making an overall assessment.[3]

Essentially, evaluation is concerned with the efficiency and effectiveness of a programme as a whole. Quite frequently, however, evaluation may deal solely with specific components such as the objectives, course content, teacher's guidance, text book, audio-visual aids, teaching methods and evaluation procedures.

4. **Curriculum Utility, Variety and Flexibility**

During the process of design and development the emphasis be laid on utility, variety and flexibility.

4.1 *Utility Criteria*

It should be noted that unless a particular concept or skill contributes directly to the achievements of one or more objectives it cannot be included in the curriculum. Individual whim, bias, likes and dislikes have no place in the curriculum design. Commonly talked 'nice to know' content and efforts be devoted to 'must know' content.

4.2 *Criteria of Variety*

Care should be taken to make a provision for interesting variety of learning experiences (inservice training, conducted planned tours, live demonstrations, laboratory situations) including instructional materials and media.

4.3 *Criteria of Flexibility*

Curriculum for different stages of education should be designed and organised in such a way that there should be provision for vertical and horizontal mobility of the students. There should be scope for a person to enter and leave the system at different points. To facilitate mobility, besides offering core subjects curriculum should also offer number of elective subjects to the students.

5. **Role of UGC in the Promotion of Curriculum Development Programme**

It has long been felt in academic circles that the programmes of studies offered at the universities in India has not kept pace with the fast changing needs and demands of the society. Such feeling has been clearly expressed in the *Programme of Action* (1986) on the national policy of education. "The courses offered by the universities have not been recognised to meet the demands of the times. Their relevance and utility are constantly questioned" (p.39). Furthermore, it says, "The credibility of the evaluation system is being eroded" (p.39). Thus the need for improvement of the curricula has been expressed clearly at national level.[4]

In addition to expressing the need for reform in the curriculum, educationists have also felt the need for introducing a certain measure of uniformity in it. Speaking on this subject, the *Challenges of Education: A Policy Perspective* (1985) draws attention to the need for "a common core curriculum to strengthen unity within diversity and to facilitate mobility from one part of the country to another" (p. 4).

Appreciating the need for continuous development and modernization of curricula and courses, UGC set-up Curriculum Development Centres (CDC's) in various subjects of study at different universities towards the close of 1985. Guidelines indicated to develop and design the curriculum by the UGC to the CDC's are as follows:

> With increasing awareness of the importance of learning process, more learner-oriented or enquiry-oriented teaching method should be introduced in the instructional system, which enables the learner to engage himself in creative and divergent thinking, problem solving, self learning and to explore new avenues of communication, productive work as well as innovation through such methods as simulation games, project work and the like. Accordingly, the main thrust of the curriculum should aim at shifting emphasis from teaching to learning, which has to be an important element in the new approach to education. This will necessitate reorganizing the curricular packages, possibly in a modular form. Greater emphasis should be placed on the students' motivation to learn than on the teacher's ability to lecture. Further, the curriculum should be so designed that it would make the education more meaningful to the needs and aspirations of its beneficiaries as well as to make it socially relevant. Students shall be encouraged to study some part of the syllabus themselves and shall be given assignments so as to make them use the library or laboratory etc.

Lectures should be supplemented by tutorials and/or problem solving sessions (which shall be around 25 per cent of the lecture workload), term paper etc, so that a student deserves the maximum benefit from his programme of study. Hence tutorials, problem solving exercises, seminars, project work etc, should form constituent parts of the proposed curricula.

Thus the curriculum centre programme was taken up by the UGC in order to promote excellence in teaching at undergraduate and post-graduate level. This is an exercise at the national level through many experts drawn from all over India. The document prepared by distinguished academics after having active interaction and thread bare discussion contains the course contents for each subject, lecture schedule, broad outlines of tutorials, problem solving exercises, practical and project work etc.

6. **Conclusion**

To conclude, the curriculum can never be static and must always change as the frontiers of knowledge expand with time. Updating and restructuring must continue to enhance the quality and standards of education. With this, it is hoped that all the institutions of higher education would be benefited and helped to achieve a more exciting pattern of education.

Keeping in view the basic considerations and the developments that are taking shape under the direction of the UGC, L&IS curriculum should always aim at training the library and information scientists and engineers with sound innovative vigour and approach. Students should be made to learn not only how of library and information science techniques but also what and why of them. Above all the designed curriculum should be in a position to kindle the enthusiasm in students about the informatin work and service.

REFERENCES

1. David, P. Curriculum *Design and Development*, New York, Harcourt Brace Jovanovich, 1980.
2. Good, C V. (ed.) *Dictionary of Education*, New Work, 1959.
3. Lewy, A. (ed.) *Handbook of Curriculum Evaluation*, Paris, Unesco and Longman, 1977.
4. Tyler, R.W. Basic Principles of Curriculum and Instruction, Chicago, University of Chicago Press, 1969.

3

SYLLABUS ANALYSIS FOR LIBRARY AND INFORMATION SCIENCE EDUCATION

A. TEJOMURTY and SUDHIR KUMAR

The three elements that are easily identified in any education system are: (a) Syllabus; (b) Teachers and students; and (c) Examinations.

Syllabus, therefore, is the dominating element in this system. The syllabus, as is understood, is a document which contains:

(a) Names of major topics;
(b) Names of secondary topics; and
(c) Time allotted.

It is desirable to provide:

(a) Statement and scope of course;
(b) Suggestions regarding teaching-learning methods and activities; and
(c) Suggestions on evaluation, techniques and tools to be used. Beside, the syllabus should also supply:

    (i) The context areas fully and clearly; and
    (ii) The intellectual abilities and skills to be developed.

The first job of a teacher is to choose and formulate instructional objectives for various lessons and units in the analysed and rearranged syllabus in a subject of study. Testing (examination) provides feedback concerning teaching effectiveness in addition to learning progress. The result reveals weaknesses of teaching learning. Instruction is to be modified suitably. Thus the syllabus is a most important part of teaching learning process.

1. New Education Policy and Syllabus

Restructuring of courses has become necessary in view of the new pattern of education which has enhanced the duration of courses leading to first degree from 14 to 15 years. New Education Policy (Programme of Action 1986) has stressed on the redesigning of higher education programmes to meet the growing demands of specialization to provide flexibility and to update and modernise curricula. In order to achieve this, it is proposed:

(i) To secure full involvement of the universities and faculties in redesigning and reorienting the courses in higher education;

(ii) To review comprehensively the existing guidelines on restructuring courses formed by the UGC to incorporate the new concepts in the design, context and structure envisaged in the policy;

(iii) To reorganise the Boards of Studies in the universities to facilitate redesigning of courses, and to promote inter-disciplinary programmes and interfaces with employment;

(iv) To organise regional and national seminars to generate enthusiasm in commitment to the new design of courses, flexibility in the combinations, modular structure, accumulation of credits etc.; and

(v) To link development grants to universities with the willingness and interest in reorganisation of courses and commitment to innovation as a continuing effort.[1]

2. Present Scene

Much stress has been laid on syllabus reorganisation in the New Educational Policy (1986). But practically the syllabus formulation, though most important, remains a totally neglected field of endeavour in the academic area. The syllabus formulation is mostly segmental, highly casual and often *ad hoc*. It is done casually, hastily and in an unrealistic way. The committees of courses or Boards of Studies discuss the issue in relation to what are the capabilities of students opting for a course. A few topics are thrown together. Sometimes it is unrealistic, impracticable and unmanageable to many teachers and students. Many a times topics are not arranged in a helpful manner — simple to complex one. It does not at all provide intellectual abilities and skills to be developed. It is silent about intention and extension of topics. It does not reveal that what, why and how a teacher has taught.

The message of the university is interpreted by different people differently. It is entirely up to the teachers to interpret the syllabus. This entirely depends on the grasp of the subject and the willingness of the teachers to work. When the message of the university is to be interpreted by every one in his own light and his willingness to decode it, the situation varies from institution to institution and from teacher to teacher. The students have to depend on the interpretation of the teachers which is often different with the paper setters and examiners.

Thus a syllabus should not be open to a teacher to interpret in anyway. The teacher should be bound by the text. The syllabus must include directions and should not be open to teachers to interpret in any other manner. Otherwise there will be no effectiveness and uniformity in instruction, and the whole teaching will be done through lecturing only, as is being done in most cases.

Syllabus is the most crucial part of the educational process. It should be able to specify in clear terms the objectives to be achieved, the contents of the course and ways to go about teaching the contents to achieve those objectives. The syllabus should have not only clarity, but also content specificity.

3. **Analysis of Syllabus**

It is necessary to analyse the syllabus to obtain its limit in clarity by subjecting it to the following questions such as:

(1) What should a teacher teach?
(2) Why should a teacher teach?
(3) How should a teacher teach?
(4) How should a teacher know what he has taught?

These basic questions have been expanded with specific items of enquiry to bring out a reasonable quantum of objectivity in the analysis by a suitable proforma.[2] listed below:

	5	4	3	2	1
1. What should a teacher teach?					
(a) All subject matter					
(b) Activity of teacher and student					
(c) Link with other subject					
(d) Depth of treatment					
2. Why should the teacher teach?					
(a) Life examples given					
(b) Students' abilities to be developed					
(c) Students' knowledge to be developed					
(d) Students' social skills to be developed					
3. How should the teacher teach?					
(a) Method of teaching					
(b) Teaching/learning aids					
(c) Time allocation					
(d) Classroom organisation					
(e) Lesson Plan					
(f) Method of evaluation					
4a. How does the teacher know what he has taught?					
(a) Type of test					
(b) Frequency of test					
4b. Syllabus indicates students'					
(a) Academic abilities					
(b) Psycho-motor skills (i.e. Perception, Adaptation and Organisation)					

4c. Laboratory achievement (if applicable)

	5	4	3	2	1
(a) Type of test					
(b) Frequency of test					

Marks obtained

Q. 1	20
Q. 2	20
Q. 3	30
Q.4 A	10
Q.4 B	10
Q.4 C	10
Grand Total	100

The rating scale is (5) very clear; (4) clear; (3) somewhat clear; (2) not clear; and (1) not at all clear. The coefficient of clarity is calculated by dividing marks gained for each question separately and for total questions. Each part of the syllabus is thus analysed and redesigned. The mark 0.20 is the desirable minimum value of coefficient of clarity. The syllabus should be modified accordingly to increase the value of the coefficient. The objective of the course and of each unit may also be suitably modified.

3.1 *Example*

1. University	:	Vikram University, Ujjain
2. Courses	:	MLIS, 1989-90
3. Paper	:	Universe of Knowledge
4. Unit	:	Concept formation, primary senses, association, intellect, intuition, and imagination; Brain chamber.
5. Experience of teacher	:	17 years

6. Experience of teaching the paper : 12 years

7. Coefficient of Clarity

1		2		3		4	
a	3	a	1	a	1	A a	1
b	2	b	2	b	1	b	1
c	2	c	3	c	1		
d	2	d	2	d	1	B a	1
				e	1	b	1
				f	2	C a	2
						b	1
Total	9		8		7		7
Maximum	20		20		30		30

Coefficient of clarity

1. 9/20 = 0.45 or 45%
2. 8/20 = 0.40 or 40%
3. 7/30 = 0.23 or 23%
4. A 2/10 = 0.20 or 20%
   B 2/10 = 0.20 or 20%
   C 3/10 = 0.30 or 30%

A+B+C =7/30 = 0.23 or 23%
Overall =31/100 = 0.31 or 31%

The overall coefficient of clarity of this unit is only 0.31 per cent which is slightly higher than the minimum value, which is 0.20. But it is not satisfactory.

3.2 *Elaboration of the Unit*

(i) Definition of the terms idea, information, concept, knowledge and subject. Interrelationship of these terms.
(ii) Definition of differentiation of terms: Intellect; intuition, imagination, their role in concept formation.
(iii) Formation of pure percepts, appercept, apperception mass and

concept, a psychological view.

(iv) Knowledge of primary senses, touch, smell, vision, hearing, methods of acquiring knowledge through these senses and ambiguities of such knowledge.

(v) Process of concept formation in brain chamber.

(vi) Formation of knowledge: Reattainment of concept, assimilation and correlation with earlier concepts, formation of an idea, information, knowledge and subject;

(vii) Time allocation: 6 clock hours

(viii) Teaching methods: Lectures, Discussions, Assignments on its application on different concepts like watch, star, crow.

(ix) Evaluation: A project, objective multiple choice testing, seminar etc.

(x) Abilities to be developed:

  (a) Use of diagrammatic representation for any concept

  (b) Impact of concept formation on designing of scheme of library classification.

REFERENCES

1. India, Higher Education (Ministry of —). National Policy on Education, 1986. Programme of Action, p 41.

2 Association of Indian Universities. Monograph on syllabus analysis and restructuring, 1984, pp 19-21.

4

RESURRECTION OF LIBRARY AND INFORMATION SCIENCE EDUCATION IN INDIA

PUSHPANJALI JENA

1. Introduction

Acquisition of knowledge and development of the intellect imply inclusion of honesty and adoption of ethical standards. The education in its real sense drives away the social evils and other malpractices, so as to bring about a considerable change in the transformation of knowledge in the human mind. This synthesization of human knowledge can be purified in the current environment through a well-established library.

2. Scope

This paper describes the present and traditional methods of library science education and suggests some changes to be adopted in the study of the subject in the competitive world in order to make the library and information science students to qualify for all varieties of jobs like students of other faculties. It also points out further that the adoption of library and information science course in schools, colleges, and universities should be at par with other subjects as a compulsory or optional subject.

3. Objectives

The basic objectives of traditional courses in the field of library and information science can be categorised in ten ways:

(i) To develop the provision for planning and proper library management;

(ii) To make the students aware of the problems of infrastructure of libraries, and train them to solve the problems by decision-making function;

(iii) To learn about statistical analysis and operational research about the day-to-day functions of libraries;

(iv) Application of information machinery system in libraries, its design and operation;

(v) To study the users' behaviour for feeding information in consonance with the current phenomenon;

(vi) To develop systematic knowledge in the field of library and information science in view of future technological developments;

(vii) To develop a strong attitude towards proper arrangement of documents for easy accessibility;

(viii) To take steps towards acquiring developed informative materials and to organise them in a scientific way so as to make reading materials available to user community with the least defined time;

(ix) To take steps for prospective growth in the field of information arrangements and to gain maximum benefits from regional and international co-operative ventures; and

(x) To take active part in the eradication of illiteracy and social evils and unethical attitude by developing library-oriented education in the society.

4. Structure of Library Science Education

The traditional system of teaching and learning which puts premium on memorization and is subordinated to examination has outlived its utility. The sole purpose of our teaching in library schools in to help the library students to pass the examination and obtain a certificate to enter the library profession. "Learning has rather become a mechanical process of acquiring skills." This soulless method of teaching and learning naturally fails to keep the students informed about the recent trends in their own professions and the new developments in the country and abroad, to meet the challenging demands of the times and to face the realities of the situation prevailing in the world of their work. This is because that academic attainments of our students is so low and poor that hardly one per cent of the library students would be able get through the various competitive examinations held in the country from time to time. Although the Library and Information Science is now a fully developed discipline and has made great strides in recent time, the library profession in India is not rated very high and it does not enjoy the same status as that of other professions.

5. New Structure of Examination

In the present century the current trend is to acquire new knowledge about new inventions. Knowledge is fast growing in every branch of science, for which a specialized study in each branch of science is necessary. The new educational policy with the following three clear-cut objectives will perhaps be very effective:

(i) Exposure to absorption of new knowledge;
(ii) Involvement in the process of education; and
(iii) Development of balanced growth of knowledge and professional aptitude.

5.1 *Exposure to Absorption of New Knowledge*

It is observed that the reading of the students of library science is generally confined to text-books only. They think that any kind of supplementary reading is unnecessary for them. They never spend their time in reading newspapers, periodicals and books of general nature unrelated to their courses of study. This exclusive dependence upon the text-book is responsible for their utter ignorance about basic facts about other subjects and the latest happenings and developments in their country and abroad. The remedial measure suggested in this connection is that the syllabus of Library and Information Science must include a paper of 100 marks about general knowledge and current affairs.

5.2 *Involvement in the Process of Education*

Proper motivation makes a student fully energetic and enthusiastic. He should be motivated not only to read the books pertaining to his profession, but also of other disciplines so as to have some knowledge about other subjects which will enable him to render library service more effectively and competently. The role of the libraries in developing reading habit among the students is very crucial. They should have all sorts of books and reference material in their collection to cater to the needs of the students. Moreover, there is also a need for continuous internal assessment of the scholastic and non-scholastic abilities of the students which certainly helps them to widen their knowledge and improve their level of attainment.

5.3 *Development of Balanced Growth of Knowledge and Professional Attitude*

The system should help to develop all-around personality of the students by emphasising the need for them to take active part in the extra-curricular and co-curricular activities. For instance they should be persuaded to participate in debate, essay competition etc. This will help them to develop an inter-disciplinary approach on a broad basis and to synthesize his knowledge. Irrespective of ones own area of study the students must be acquainted with the fundamentals of other branches of knowledge.

6. **Present Position**

During recent times the educational system of our country has gone a sea change. Of late it is being realised that school students should be apprised about the rudiments of the library science. As a matter of fact there is a proposal that the subject of library science should be included as an optional subject in the courses of study in the higher secondary schools. But it is difficult to say at present when this proposal would be materialised.

In +2 courses, library science must be treated as a group subject and a honours subject in three-year degree course. In some of the colleges, library science is being studied as an extra optional subject.

7. **Recent Trends**

It is now widely believed that L&IS education should be of two-year post-graduate course as one-year course fails to enable the students to have adequate acquaintance and grasp of the subject. The longer period of study of the subject has a good deal of advantages from the point of view of Katherine Packer.

7.1 A longer period helps to cover the fundamentals and develop specialized knowledge.

7.2 Being studied in under-graduate level the students will be able to have an idea on the contents of the subject.

7.3 Being engaged for five years, students will get more time for practical work. But Mr. F. William Summers, Dean, University of South Carolina College of Library and Information Science, does not subscribe to this view. He maintains that longer period of study means higher cost with no proof of benefits. Moreover, there seems to be no convincing evidence for the two-year degree courses to produce better librarians. The very question of specialization in the first year degree course also is doubtful.

8. Suggestions

8.1 It is observed that the subject library science is considered among faculties of Arts. But when the subject is open for science students, Library and Information Science may be considered as an optional subject for + 2 science students. After that the +2 science students can study L&IS as an honours subject in +3 degree course in case they so desire.

8.2 The course of study which is to be prepared for library and information science at the level of post-graduate study should include one foreign language as one of the papers. The very intention behind it is that the post-graduate students are likely to be absorbed in libraries, and they have to scan foreign journals and books, which they can do themselves without the help of translations.

8.3 There must be a workshop on the generation and management of a small scale data base analysis of current information in each year.

8.4 Regional workshop on the use of computers in cataloguing and classification and other fields of Library Science may be conducted for the further growth of knowledge.

8.5 The practice of donations for securing admission to professional courses is an unhealthy and undesirable practice. In the case of Library and Information Science this should be strongly discouraged.

8.6 The M.Phil course as a refresher-oriented media may be developed in the field of L&IS just like in other subjects.

8.7 The new national core curriculum must be implemented at national level in order to educate all the library professionals in a proportionate manner and make them fit for any set-up.

8.8 National Information System may be developed.

5

UNIT PATTERN OF SYLLABUS WITH SPECIAL REFERENCE TO LIBRARY AND INFORMATION SCIENCE SUBJECT FOR B.A/B.SC. DEGREE COURSES

A.K. BARADOL

1. Introduction

The University of Madras started the first full time post-graduate diploma course in library science of one academic year duration in 1937. The Master's and Doctorate programme were added later on. The structure of library and information science education in the universities was framed about half century back in India. The same structure for the first course in library science education has been continued with a change in the nomenclature of the course from 'Diploma' in the universities in India.

2. Present Position of the Provision of Library Science Subject for B.A/B.Sc

Since the beginning of the last decade, library science education is being imparted at degree level also. Degree is referred here as a general degree like B.A/B.Sc, not the Bachelor of Library Science. In Orissa State at S.B. Women's College, Cuttack, library science subject has been introduced in the first half of 1970's at the graduation level. Bishop Hebber College, Trichirappalli (Tamil Nadu), an autonomous institute, has started the B.A in library science in the first half of 1980's.

3. Need

For providing the para professionals for library and information work, the country needs the B.A/B.Sc graduates who have also acquired the library and information science knowledge along with other subjects. The professionals have already thought over this issue. At different seminars/conferences/symposia this issue has been discussed and resolutions have been passed to that effect. To quote from the Seminar Resolutions, "It has also been resolved to request the authorities to introduce Library and Information Science and allied courses at undergraduate (plus 2 level) and graduate levels (plus 3) as major minor (optional) courses".[1] In this direction the Mangalore University in Karnataka has initiated a plan which is under submission to the state government for its approval.

4. Advantages of L&IS Subject for B.A/B.Sc

The students who complete the B.A/B.Sc degree with the library and information science subject would study for two or three years other optional subjects also. In each university the total number of optionals varies. This facilitates the student to take up two years' master's degree programme in Library and Information Science. If he wishes, he can also study any other subject at the master's level. If the introduction of the two years integrated master's degree in library and information science is delayed, the student can be admitted to the existing one year BLISc course. They may be given preference in the admission.

The persons who are interested in getting training for any semi-professional library positions can manage with only B.A/B.Sc degree. In the present pattern he is required to complete the Diploma which will not earn a degree to him.

5. Unit Pattern of Syllabus

The Library and Information Science (L&IS) syllabus in all courses provides for an overall choice in each paper. The over all choice provides the students a chance to answer any five or six questions out of eight, nine or ten. This can be replaced by a new pattern where the library and information science students shall be required to answer each of several alternate questions.

The Library and Information Science syllabus of each paper shall be demarcated by the Board of Studies or Select Committees, into well defined units or areas of contents. The syllabus of each paper has to be broken down into different units.

5.1 *The Numbering of Units*

In the new pattern of syllabus each unit or area in each subject has to be numbered using Indo-Arabic numerals or Roman numerals. The alphabets can be used instead of Indo-Arabic numerals or Roman numbers.

5.2 *Choice*

(A) *Theory*: The student in the present pattern in all the library and information science examinations gets a choice of questions. The choice given to the students in difficult to withdraw.
(B) *Practical*: In the practical examinations in some universities there is no choice. To cite the instances, in the Mangalore University, Gulbarga, and the Karnatak University, Dharwad, the L&IS students are required to classify or catalogue all the given documents by CC and DC or UDC as the case may be. The choice in the proposed new pattern is in the units or areas. In the question paper the choice is to be provided by alternate questions on each unit or the area of the subject.

The student will be left with no choice except reading all the units or areas of all the subjects. This forces the student to know the subject very well in a thorough manner.

5.3 *Model Question Paper*

The students have to be informed about the new pattern of question papers well in advance. Otherwise there is a danger of students getting upset by looking to the new type of question papers. For each paper the model questions paper has to be prepared.

5.4 *The Initiation*

The initiation in this regard has to be made by a teachers of L&IS. The initiation may be done by the Chairman of Board of Studies in L&IS. Or even the members of Boards of Studies in L&IS can move the resolutions to this effect in their own universities. Once this is approved the Board of Studies in L&IS at the different universities or the Board of Technical Education of Vocational Education, or the other bodies will approve.

6. The Model

The following optional papers can be offered to the B.A/B.Sc degree courses. Each university in India has its own regulations governing the B.A/B.Sc degree programme. Hence the Board of Studies of the different universities can modify the total number of papers etc. as per the rules and regulations of B.A/B.Sc of the universities. The list of books can be provided by the Board of Studies. Hence the following syllabus does not include the list of books.

Each paper can be of 100 Marks. Marks for internal assessment may be 30 and marks for examination may be 70. Each unit can have 10 marks. A question can be asked from each unit of area of the paper with an alternative.

I. Title of the paper: Fundamentals of Library Science

Units	*Topic*
1	Library and Society
2	Laws of library science
3	Types of libraries and their functions
4	Educational functions and social functions
5	Principles of library management
6	Library routines - selection, acquisition
7	Library routines - processing, display, circulation, and maintenance.

II. Title of the paper: Information Sources and Services

Units	*Topic*
1	Objectives and functions of reference work and reference service
2	Types of reference works – Bibliographies, dictionaries, and Encyclopedias etc.
3	Primary sources of information – Periodicals, Conference proceedings, Theses and dissertations, Standards and specifications.

4 Secondary sources of information – Abstracting and indexing, and bibliographies.
5 Tertiary sources – Bibliography of Bibliographies.
6 Abstracting services.
7 Current awareness services

III. Title of the paper: Classification Theory

Units	*Topic*
1	Nature and purpose of library classification
2	History of classification
3	Main features of DDC and CC
4	Basic concepts of Colon Classification
5	General theory of library classification
6	Canons, postulates, and principles
7	Notation and devices.

IV. Title of the paper: Cataloguing Theory

Unit	*Topic*
1	Nature and purpose of library cataloguing
2	History of cataloguing codes – CCC and AACR
3	Physical forms and functions of library catalogue.
4	Varieties of entries
5	Subject headings
6	Methods and rules of filing catalogue cards
7	Cooperation – Centralised and union catalogue

V. Title of the paper: Classification Practicals

Construction of call numbers for simple, compound and complex documents by latest version of DDC and CC for seven documents/titles.

VI Title of the paper : Cataloguing Practice

Preparation of catalogue entries according to latest editions of CCC and AACR for seven documents.

7. Conclusion

In the paper it is suggested to introduce the L&IS subject for B.A/B.Sc degree. If implemented it has the following implications and issues to be discussed and arrived at a decision. They are:

(a) Eligibility for admission to Master's degree in L&IS;
(b) The possible preference in Master's degree in L&IS admission to be given to the degree holders with L&IS subjects,
(c) The change of recruitment rules to para professionals/semi-professional positions in the libraries.

The standardisation of L&IS education at B.A/B.Sc level has to be aimed. There will be financial difficulties in the introduction of L&IS subjects for degree courses. The main problem will be the salary for the L&IS teachers in the colleges. In the initial stages the college librarians who possess the MLIS degree may be requested to teach the B.A/B.Sc students. It is possible to introduce the L&IS subjects to B.A/B.Sc degree by the joint efforts of professionals and educational administrators of the universities and colleges.

REFERENCE

1. Seminar on restructuring the course and introduction of two-year integrated programme of MLISc course. Osmania University, Hyderabad, September 1986, *Resolutions*.

6

KNOWLEDGE AND SKILLS FOR SECONDARY INFORMATION WORK AND SERVICE: Foundation of Curricula and Syllabi

GANESH BHATTACHARYA

1. Introduction

Since the beginning of 1970's the information service profession has been witnessing a considerable amount or rethinking and activities relating to the development of manpower for information work and service. This rethinking and activities were prompted by a social pressure mostly created by changes in social attitudes towards the role of information in national development; and by the development of technologies that can be profitably utilized to exploit the information resources for the purpose of national development. The study of the source-documents embedding the results of those rethinking provided an opportunity to develop a generalized model pertaining to the systematization of different, essential programme components of a system for the development of manpower for information work and service. The model specified the different responsible agencies and a full complement of programmes at different levels that could ensure the required quality and quantity. It had substantial portion devoted to the question of knowledge and skills for information work and service. However, it was the result of a macro-analysis of the problem. It holds good still today. But, a special need has arisen now for a micro-analysis of the problem in the context of the emerging information society; and to identify the matching knowledge and skills required for information work and service to meet the information-needs of the society. It may be noted here that the paper entitled "Information

Society and Information Service Profession",[1] discusses in detail the implications of the emerging information society for the information service profession by enumerating the characteristic features of the information society and the desirable professional attributes of information service professionals. In a sense, this paper is a complement to the other paper in answering the question about the necessary and sufficient knowledge and skill for information work and service in the emerging information society.

2. Essential Message of the Information Society

The term 'Information Society" refers to an information-intensive society that is gradually emerging. The majority of the members of this society are gradually developing a confidence of self-reliance in the matter of problem solving by utilizing existing pertinent information, as much as feasible, through personal efforts, and they have started believing without any hesitation that there is pertinent information available for this purpose which they can get access to when they need it. They are realizing the importance of life-long learning; and in all these matters they are relying heavily on advances in technologies. By implications, they are gradually becoming self-reliant depending heavily upon the information services. Getting access to right information at the right time is possible if and only if there is a massive collection of information well-organized, stored, and provided with user-friendly means of getting access to it. One can be self-reliant in solving his own problem by using information; but none can be self-reliant in the matter of massive work involved in making right information accessible to users. Obviously therefore, the information service professionals should take advantage of the emerging situation. But for that purpose, they are to equip themselves in a way quite distinct from the conventional way. In the matter of equipping themselves, the predominant question is "What knowledge; and what skills?.

3. Procedure for Selecting Knowledge and Skills

Knowledge and skills are acquired through professional education and training. The education and training for a particular profession may have to be of different levels for reasons of economy, efficiency, and effectiveness of professional activities. Besides, it may call for the development of para-professionals for similar reasons. The education and training for information work and service is a typical example of the type mentioned above. For this reason, it is necessary to work out a systematic procedure for selecting knowledge and skills for different levels of education and training. The very purposes of distinguishing the levels of professional education and training suggests the following procedure.

(i) Scan the predominant environments to ascertain the information needs of the users in different environments, and also the types of information services needed to meet these information needs;

(ii) Mark out the professional work and services that call for advanced professional competence;

(iii) Select the necessary and sufficient knowledge and skills that are warranted to display advanced professional competence. This is for a course of advanced level;

(iv) Mark out the areas that warrant further specialization at the advanced level considering the requirements of various environments. This is for courses of specialization after the course of advanced level;

(v) If it is warranted for the sake of economy, efficiency, and effectiveness, select the necessary and sufficient knowledge and skills essential for extending professional assistance to the professionals performing information work and services of advanced level. This is for a level of course immediately lower than the advanced level; and

(vi) If it is warranted for the sake of economy, efficiency and effectiveness, decide about the necessary and sufficient knowledge and skills required for extending assistance to the professionals in their professoinally routine tasks. This is for a course for developing para-professional manpower.

This paper aims at identifying the necessary and sufficient knowledge and skills required for performing information work and rendering information services at the advanced level in different environments at the moment and in the near future.

4. Factors Warranting Consideration

In any matured profession it is not at all difficult to recognize the "contributors" to the development of the discipline that forms the foundation of the concerned profession. These contributors emerge from among the practitioners, teachers, and researchers of the profession. They display their professional competence in their work; and they gain recognition. Their works reveal to a large extent the knowledge and skills they are equipped with. The selection of knowledge and skills for the purpose of designing professional course of advanced level are largely influenced by this finding either directly or indirectly. For this reason, this is, indeed, the most important single factor that warrants consideration. But, in essence, it consists of several sub-factors. We may look into them by taking the example of information service profession.

The profession of information service professionals is a matured profession. It has s large number of "contributors" both past and present, covering a century of its development. If we analyse their works, we find that their conception of "profession" is profound, and they succeed admirably well in distinguishing the professional contents of the discipline of library science, documentation and information science. In their approach towards any professional problem, they display clearly, a distinct mode of thinking which may be designated today as systems-approach. This implies that any centre for rendering information services may be regarded as a service production system. Its problems are analogous to any such system; and they warrant systems-approach for their solutions. As a result of systems-thinking, they are in a position to appreciate the changes in the conception of each and every component of any level of the information service system – whether it is a library, or a documentation/information centre, or an information analysis and consolidation centre, or a data centre. It is because of this approach, they are highly appreciative of the scientific management techniques for the design, development, organisation, operation, control, and evaluation of the information service system. As a result, they develop high managerial capability. To them, the rules-of-procedure for any professional activity are extremely important as they are always purpose-oriented. They always try to demonstrate their derivation from generalized principles. In their expression of professional ideas, they prefer standardized terminology. The whole set of rules-of-procedure for different professional activities are their professional software technology. The tools associated with rules of procedure are of great importance to them. They have been prescribing all-along the use of the appropriate hardware technology that ensures increased productivity giving demonstration of their use.

The problems covered by them belong to a wide range of practices of information services at the root of which a number of applied disciplines are traceable. The way they deal with those problems shows their profound knowledge of the fundamental disciplines forming the foundations of those applied disciplines. The results of their researches clearly show their deep knowledge of "Research Methodology". In their research, they make use of selected portions (knowledge) of other disciplines, such as, logic, mathematics, statistics, etc. They are their tool-subjects for carrying out research. In addition, we find that they want us to realize that "Information" as a concept is quite abstract. It becomes concrete only when it is information on some subject (discipline) or another. To carry out information work and service, it is essential to have necessary and sufficient knowledge of the concerned subject. It is not the same knowledge of the subject that is required for carrying out research in it; but it is knowledge of certain facets of the subject for carrying out information work and services on it, and to enter into a meaningful dialogue with the specialists in the subject to ascertain their information needs.

Above all, we find that all their knowledge and skills through the process of their systems-approach culminate into a generalized "philosophy" of the discipline of their practice. This philosophy integrates all the branches of the discipline and can answer the why, what, and how of the information service system by taking into account its environment, objective, input, throughput, and output. It is interesting to note that the knowledge and skills that the "Contributors" acquire, largely by their personal efforts, and ultimately get recognition make them adequately "flexible" in their learning endeavours. They can recognize easily what new things they should learn; and they can learn it with minimum efforts. This capability is essential to be a participant in the life-long learning.

Our intention is to develop manpower for secondary information work and services of high standard (advanced level). The contributors of our professional discipline will emerge out of this manpower. The education system for our profession must provide all that is necessary and sufficient for creating its foundation. Therefore, it becomes imperative for us to consider these factors in selecting the knowledge and skills needed for this purpose. This is essential in the context of the emerging information society.

For every profession, there is and there should be a manpower development system in the true sense of the term. A model system for developing manpower for information work and service has been suggested in a paper entitled "Development of Professional Manpower for Information Service: A Model"[2] The ultimate objective of this system is to covert the appropriate man (input) through appropriate method of enriching him with appropriate knowledge and skills (throughput) into an appropriate manpower for information work and services (output). This is the essential implication of the term 'Development' in manpower development. Here, we are primarily concerned with the knowledge and skills of this manpower. The consideration of the factors mentioned above suggests the appropriate knowledge and skills required for this purpose.

5. Appropriate Knowledge and Skills

Furnished below is the list of appropriate knowledge and skills that the factors considered above would suggest. The arguments in favour of their recognition are to a large extent obvious. However, wherever, necessary, some notes have been added. It may be noted here that no attempt has been made here to organise the knowledge and skills into papers for a course. That is a separate question. But one point must be taken note of. The implications of the information-intensive society would suggest the implementation of the principle of "life-long learning" for the information service professionals also. This is, indeed, a highly potent principle. It can dictate terms about all aspects of education for information work and service. They include the:

1. Levels of courses;
2. Course contents;
3. Duration;
4. Entry qualifications;
5. Teaching/Learning techniques;
6. Evaluation procedures and techniques;
7. Strategies and forms of continuing education programmes; and even the
8. Display mechanisms of professional behaviour.

Behind all these aspects of professional education and training lies the selection of knowledge and skills required for information work and service at the advanced level.

5.1 *Appropriate Knowledge and Skills*

(i) Knowledge of systems-approach and the skills of applying it. (*Note*: This is the most appropriate mode of thinking applicable to any aspects of information service systems including their environments, super systems, objectives, sub-systems (components), coordinate systems, and the functional and structural relationships between and among components. The results obtained by its application are most useful in designing or planning, developing, organizing, operating, controlling, understanding, explaining, and evaluating an information service system and all its components, whether they are entities or attributes, or functions).

(ii) Knowledge of the philosophy of information science and the skills of using it in all professional attitudes and activities. (*Note*: The term 'Philosophy' in this case refers to the organized body of knowledge that answers the questions of why, what, and how of information science and systems. It should necessarily comprehend all the working concepts, postulates, principles, and the rules of procedure that unify all the major components (branches) of information science that forms the scope and status of information science revealing the scope and status of information science that forms the foundation of information service systems showing its intimate relationship with information generation and utilization systems, and primary information communication systems. The term "Information Science" should necessarily refer to the study of primary information as a phenomenon to the extent useful for secondary information services; and specially to the study of all the information service phenomena).

(iii) Knowledge of (1) Information as a resource phenomenon; (2) Use of information; (3) Users of Information; (4) Information service profession, professionals and their educational programmes; (5) Information service systems, centres, and programmes; and (6) Environments of information generation, communication and services (e.g. information and society, institutions, organizations, governments etc.,) and; the skill of applying this knowledge in developing professional tools, techniques, and services; and in information resource and service management. (*Note*: From the point of view of research, these may be regarded as fundamental disciplines as the knowledge in these areas are largely generated by oriented fundamental research. Knowledge in these areas are effectively used in the applied disciplines devoted to the following information work and services: (1) Dissemination of news about research in progress; (2) Preparation of indexes and other aids to primary information embedded in individual documents; (3) Dissemination and retrieval of information about, comparatively current, micro documents, and making provision of access to those documents (in a narrow sense, technically known as "Documentation"; (4) Preparation of non-critical factual documents, e.g. state-of-the art reports, space-profiles, time-profiles, process-profiles, product-profiles, etc.; (5) Trading of documents (Book selling); (6) Acquisition, organization storage, dissemination, and retrieval of information about macro documents, service of macro documents and preservation of documents (traditionally known as "Library Science"); (7) "Archive Science"; (8) Reprographic service; and (9) Translation service.

(iv) Knowledge of communication channels or media, and of the sources of information (reference, primary, secondary, etc.), and the skills of generating and rendering information services based on those.

(v) Knowledge of the professional techniques, tools, and services such as (1) Techniques for collection development; (2) Surrogating – that is, classification, cataloguing, indexing, storing; and (3) Repackaging – that is, abstracting, extracting, digesting, and analysis and consolidation (technical writing); (4) of tools, such as, manuals, codes, standards, and control devices; and (5) of the information services – that is, reference service, dissemination service, retrieval service etc; and the skills of applying this knowledge in designing, developing, and improving the techniques and tools; and in designing information for dissemination and retrieval.

(vi) Knowledge of the use of appropriate technologies, such as, computer, telecommunication, and graphic technologies including reprographic technologies to the extent necessary and sufficient; and the skills of applying this knowledge in housekeeping operations and in information storage, dissemination, retrieval, and other information services.

(vii) Knowledge of scientific management of a service production system; and the skills of applying this knowledge in the management of information service system, centres, and programme. (*Note*: The term "Management"' in terms of operations, refers primarily to planning, designing, developing, organizing, operating, controlling and evaluating. All of them involve decision-making by considering all possible alternatives. They pertain to the inputs, throughput, and outputs of the information service systems. In specific terms, they manifest as manpower management financial management, material management, equipment management, process management, product management, etc.)

(viii) Knowledge of appropriate research methodologies applicable to the area of information service systems; and the skills of applying it in doing research in the field, and in evaluating other research results to determine their usefulness in one's own field of professional interest. (*Note*: It is well known that the knowledge of research methodologies in absolute term is not adequate for its applications. It calls for the knowledge of appropriate portions of several other too-disciplines. Some of the tool-discipline, the portions of which have been found useful in relations to information service systems, are as follows: (1) General systems theory; (2) Logic; (3) Mathematics; (4) Statistics; (5) Operations research; (6) Linguistics; and (7) Psychology. In addition, "Technical Report Writing" is now consideration as an integral part of research methodologies. Knowledge of this discipline and the skills of applying this is essential for preparing products of information analysis and consolidation).

(ix) Knowledge of a methodology of studying subjects (disciplines) for information work and service; and the skills of using it whenever the need arises in the profcssional career. (*Note*: For the sake of professional interest, it becomes imperative to define "Information" in neutral term. One such definition is as follows: "Information is the message conveyed or intended to be conveyed by a systematized body of ideas". In practical professional life, there is nothing like neutral information. Any information must pertain to some subject (discipline – an organised body of knowledge that admits of study and research) or another. The primary concern of an information service professional is the information work and service predominantly pertaining to a subject or a group of subjects. His professional work calls for necessary and sufficient knowledge of some of the special facets of the subjects he is concerned with. This knowledge is not the knowledge in depth that is required for doing research in the concerned subjects. Besides, there is hardly any scope of acquiring knowledge of these special facets of the concerned subjects in the academic courses in colleges and universities. This aspect of professional knowledge has been discussed thoroughly in the paper entitled "Project on study of subjects".[3] Without going into details of it, it can be asserted here that no professional can learn all these facets of all the major subjects before entering into his professional job; it is humanly impracticable. Therefore, the solution lies only in his learning a methodology of studying subjects for information work and service, so that he can use his skills in his professional career whenever the need arises. Obviously, the method should be such that it ensures all possible economy, efficiency and effectiveness. To develop the skill of applying it, one has to choose a subject that one can handle comfortably. A subject of one's academic study satisfies this criterion. One has to carry out a project to develop this skill. The contents of learning include the following:

(a) The definition(s) of the term(s) denoting the subject, its terminological development, if any, and its scope in terms of its major divisions and subdivisions, subjects using it, and the subjects used by it;
(b) Classification of the subject including academic and documentary classifications;
(c) Development of the subject in terms of its major landmarks, trend in research, and trend in education;
(d) Sources of information pertaining to the subject including documentary, institutional and human sources; and
(e) Information transfer processes relating to the subject.

The knowledge and skills acquired by carrying out the project on study of subjects becomes adequate to start and carry out information work and service in the subject quite efficiently. However, the quality of this knowledge and skills can be improved upon by carrying out suitable professional project work during the course itself. The projects that have been found most suitable for this purpose and also for improving upon other professional knowledge and skills are discussed in the following section.

6. **Development of Professional Skills**

All the areas of knowledge mentioned in the earlier section are associated with their corresponding skills. It is essential to make provision of adequate "Practice Sessions" within the course itself, specially wherever they are warranted to help development of skills. To improve upon the majority of skills mentioned in the earlier section, it is also essential, specially for courses of advanced level, to provide scope for doing professional work and service projects. Two such projects have been found very effective in this regard. They call for the application of all professional techniques. The subject on which the professional techniques are to be applied should fall within the purview of the discipline chosen for studying subject for information work and service. In that case, the project work will definitely be of high standard. At the same time, it will intensify the subject knowledge of the project worker giving him the opportunity of improving upon his skill.

One of the projects should be the designing of a vocabulary control device on the concerned subject. The other would consist of writing a state-of-the-art report on current research in the concerned subject. It may be mentioned here that one of the effective methods for developing subject-knowledge is to enter into a meaningful dialogue with subject specialists in regard to ascertaining their information needs. The knowledge acquired by studying the concerned subject for information work and services goes a long way in the matter of entering into such meaningful dialogue. To carry out the two projects during the course itself, the project worker has to consult the subject-specialists. All these consultations augment the subject-knowledge for information work and service. By carrying out all these professional projects during the course, the course participants develop adequate skills in applying all the professional techniques including the technique of applying the methodology of studying subjects for information work and service.

7. **Conclusion**

The society that is gradually emerging along with a so-called revolution in certain fields of technology, namely, computer technology, has already been designated as "Information Society". It is going to be visible very soon in the developing countries. The profession engaged in a secondary information work and service in the developing countries must take note of the characteristic features of this society to initiate progressive changes as a preparation to face the challenge in the near future. The most important in this preparation, is the decision about the professional course-contents of the advanced level of our educational and training programmes. In more concrete terms, it amounts to asking "what knowledge and skills are appropriate for us in information work and services?" The answer to this question emerges out of an integration of our own experiences with the implications of the advances in technology.

REFERENCES

1. Bhattacharyya, G., Information society and information service profession, *DRTC Silver Jubilee Seminar*, 1987, Paper AK.
2. Bhattacharyya, G., Development of professional manpower for information service: A model. *Journal of Library and Information Science*. 4(2); 1979, Dec., 127-143.
3. Bhattacharyya, G., Project on study of subject, *Library Science with a Slant to Documentation*, 12; 1975; Paper G.

7

PRACTICAL TRAINING IN LIBRARY AND INFORMATION SCIENCE EDUCATION: Need for an All India Policy

N. LAXMAN RAO

1 Introduction

Library Science education had celebrated its centenary in 1987. In India, Library Science education can be traced from 1911-1912, when the first training course was started in Baroda by W.A.Borden. After this several associations, universities, polytechnics, autonomous institutions had started the training programmes.

The training programmes are offered at different levels such as post-Matric, post-Inter and post-Graduation levels.

Various levels of Courses, the duration and the sponsoring agencies are given in the following[1]:

Course level	Sponsoring Agengies	Duration of the course
CLSc	—Library Associations —Colleges —Universities	6-12 months
Diploma	—Polytechnics —Library Associations —Universities	1 to 2 years
Undergraduate Courses (as elective/optionals)	—Universities —Colleges	3 years
Degree Courses	—Universities	1 year
Masters Course	-do-	1 to 2 years
M.Phil.	-do-	-do-

Ph.D.	-do-	3 years
Associateship in Information Science	—Autonomous Institutions	1 year teaching and 1 year dissertation
Inservice/ refresher/short-term courses	—Libraries/Documentation Centres, Associations, Colleges and Universities	No specified period

Three levels of courses are popular and conducted by more than one kind of institutions. They are:

Certificate	–	for Semi-professional level
Degree	–	for Professional level
P.G.	–	for Professional and senior Professional level.

2. **Objectives of L&IS Education**

The University Grants Commission review Committee in its report had recommended the following objectives:

1. To give the student an understanding of the basic principles and fundamental laws of Library Science;
2. To enable the student to understand and appreciate the functions and purposes of a library in the changing social and academic set-up of the society; and
3. To train the student in the techniques of librarianship and management of libraries.

Further, Isaac had stated that the goal of Library and Information Science education is the preparation of personnel for the task of successful performance at different types of libraries with an insight into the role of these libraries in a fast changing society. He further emphasized that during the period of education the trainee should be thoroughly grounded upon the intellectual foundation of the profession and attain the competence in the technical and technological skills required for their day to day practice in different positions.

These objectives are the basis for designing the course contents and also training method.

3. **Training Methods**

The training methods followed by various schools as seen and studied by Isaac are:

1. Lecture-cum-discussion
2. Practical Work
3. Case Study Method
4. Field/Observation work
5. Tutorial
6. Assignment
7. Seminar/Colloquiums
8. Study Tour

All these methods are followed with varied emphasis. Lecture-cum-discussion is the main method followed by almost all the schools. Other methods support the trainee to supplement the class room teaching as well as make him to learn intensively. It also provides an opportunity to have 'hands on experience'.

4. **Practical Work**

Librarian's job is a professional one. To be a professional, one has to learn the skills and techniques in the profession, required to be applied/used in the daily routine work. To learn the skills and techniques, lecture method is not at all sufficient. The observation techniques may be further advantageous to lectures and discussion. But it does not provide full knowledge of skills and techniques. Further, 'hands on experience' is necessary to work in any library. The practical work gives confidence to trainees to work in any capacity such as semi-professional/professional.

Bansal and Tikku observed that practical work is necessary to bridge the gap between theory and practice and to cultivate skills through practice. Theoretical insight and practical experience are essentially different things which complement each other but neither can act as substitute for the other.

Motivale and Jagtar Singh had stated that education, if it is to be effective, has to be substantiated by a lot of practice relating to different techniques, operations and technologies of the profession.

Further, the following reasons also underline need for inclusion of practical work in library science education.

1. The trainees/students are fresh candidates. Just theoretical lectures do not make them understand and subsequently practice the different techniques used in libraries;
2. Within the limited time of one or two academic years, one has to learn a number of subjects;
3. The trainee has to join in a library after completion of his training. The librarian/administrator generally insists for practical knowledge while recruiting the library personnel. If no practical work is involved during the training period, the candidate may need sufficient time to take up the job;
4. Practical work gives confidence to the trainee to handle the jobs assigned;
5. It also gives an opportunity to understand the local variations; and
6. It supports and strengthens class-room teaching.

5. **Present Status**

Isaac has identified that the practical work prominently figures in classification, cataloguing, reference service and book selection. Practical work in cataloguing and classification is included in the syllabus of all the universities. This constitutes 25 per cent of the BLISc Course Contents. Visit to libraries, study tours and observation work are not part of the course in all the universities. Some universities do train the students in preparation of bibliographies also.·Emphasis on practical training is necessary but how to include this training? However, the practical training can be ,made possible by making the trainee to work in a library as a part of requirement in obtaining the qualification/certificate in the regular academic programmes.

6. **Apprenticeship**

Every trainee should be asked to gain practical experience. The stages of gaining experience are: (1) before joining the course, (2) during the course, and (3) after completion of the course.[2]

First category is not helpful as the trainees will not be able to learn and practice all the techniques taught during the training period. The second category may be difficult due to limitation of time. During this period the trainee will be preparing for the examinations and the concentration will be on the examinations rather than on practical work. The practical training after the course for a specified period will help the trainee to put all his time and energy in learning process.

Amitab Chatterjee suggested that every student should undergo a minimum period of practical training in any recognised institution as an internee or apprentice before being granted the certificate or the degree. All the skills and techniques are not used in one library, hence the trainee may be asked to work in more than one library to gain practical experience in different areas techniques. The need and importance of practical training is felt by library science schools and the librarians since a long time. This can be enforced if a National Policy is formulated.

7. National Policy

There is a need for national policy for Library Science education. The UGC is supposed to be the most suitable organization to take up formulation of such policy. UGC has to prepare a model syllabus, which should include the practical training after the course, as a pre-requisite for awarding the certificate. This model syllabus has to be enforced in all the library science schools in India.

UGC has already taken up 'Curriculum Development Centres' programme in order to promote excellence in teaching at undergraduate and post-graduate level. This is an exercise at national level through many experts drawn from all over India. UGC has to establish one such Centre for Library Science and be entrusted with the responsibility of looking after the preparation of model curriculum.[3]

8. Conclusion

(1) A national policy has to be evolved/formulated for L&IS Education in the changing context of librarianship in modern India, under various kinds of establishments with varied functions and responsibilities. Such policy should emphasize the need for practical training.

(2) The policy should insist that every trainee should work in a recognized library as an internee/apprentice for a specified period of three to six months.

(3) UGC has to establish a Curriculum Development Centre in Library Science to prepare model syllabus.

REFERENCES

1. Mangla, P.B. (ed.), *Library and Information Science Education in India*, Delhi, Macmillan, 1981.
2. Kumar, P.S.G. (ed.), Hundred years of library science education and its future. *Seminar Volume*, Nagpur, Nagpur University, 1987.
3. Report of the Curriculum Development Centre in Chemistry, Delhi, UGC, 1989.

8

DEVELOPMENT OF CURRICULUM DESIGN WITH A SLANT TO THE ANALYSIS OF COURSE CONTENT IN BLIS SYLLABI PURSUED IN WEST BENGAL LIBRARY SCHOOLS

S.K. CHATTERJEE

1. **Introduction**

Library and Information Science education is largely a twentieth century phenomenon. It is a professional education which brings efficiency, competency, confidence, leadership of personnel. But it is often pointed out that education offered in the library schools is unrelated to the realities of library work and this split has been termed as 'Ivory Tower Syndrome'. The courses conducted in various library schools is not in conformity with the present situation. We are now moving to a relatively new concept, namely, 'Information Society'. In fact, we live in what Alvin Toffler calls inforo-sphere in which all information, past and present – produced anywhere and everywhere in the world constitutes a vital resource as energy, minerals and the like. Hence, in this new environment the library and information services have become an essential component of all activities of man on earth. This service can be enhanced by the development of the curriculum content.

2. **Definition of Curriculum**

Curriculum is defined as the organized whole of learning experiences provided by an educational institution to bring about the desired changes in the learners. It must be liberal enough to accommodate a radical reconstruction and reformulation of the objectives of education and also to cover the introduction of new methods of teaching and learning.

2.1 *Foundations of Curriculum Development*

The development of curriculum is shaped by certain factors. Aims of formal education form the foundation for the development of curriculum. Research is essential for inhibiting unhealthy trends from influencing the curriculum.

Another foundation for curriculum development is the scientific understanding of culture. Educational goals which are achieved through curriculum development in various disciplines need to be in conformity with broad cultural goals. The breakdown from hollow traditions "to develop better values" is fundamental to curriculum development.

The third foundation on which curriculum is built is the phenomenon of learning. In order to develop a curriculum, a knowledge about the nature of man and the nature of learning is essential. It is necessary to revise the curriculum in the light of new knowledge derived from theories.

The fourth foundation for curriculum development is the nature of knowledge. The contents of knowledge to be used in teaching can be divided into several levels. These levels are facts, concepts, principles, generalizations, methods, processes and criteria.

The levels of knowledge facilitate integration in curriculum. The levels help to determine sequence in content. Knowledge has to be divided into some meaningful categories to bring order out of knowledge explosion and the need for specialization today, because the universe of knowledge is expanding very fast today.

2.2 *Dimensions of Curriculum Development*

The development of curriculum can be studied in terms of three dimensions as suggested by Lulla.[1] These are: (a) Curriculum planning; (b) Curriculum implementation; (c) Curriculum evaluation.

The effectiveness of curriculum development depends on the effectiveness of each of its three dimensions. The teacher of L&IS needs to be given guidance as well as freedom in making decisions about educational objectives, contents, and learning experience for the course he is asked to teach.

But, in reality, it is found that the syllabi, text-books, and curriculum guides are often not updated in the light of new knowledge in subject matter and new methods of teaching. There is an educational and cultural lag between the syllabi and text-books on the one hand, and the current subject matter and methods of teaching, on the other. The curriculum, thus, is not properly followed. A proper implementation of curriculum is dependent on the effectiveness of the teacher in selecting objectives and learning experiences as well as on the syllabi and text-books provided to him.

The evaluation of curriculum is possible only when the evaluation is carried out systematically to bring about an improvement in the educational programme. Decisions about curriculum evaluation should be finalised only after a qualified person is assigned to do this job.

2.3 *Process of Curriculum Development*

The task of developing a curriculum involves several steps. The sequence of these steps need to be logically determined. The following steps determine the curriculum development in L&IS education:

(a) Selection, formulation, and classification of objectives;
(b) Selection and organization of learning experiences;
(c) Evaluation of learning; and
(d) Implementation of evaluation results.

Objectives in any curriculum are the educational purpose towards which all educational efforts are directed. The curriculum planners need to develop an inter-disciplinary approach in selecting objectives. The L&IS educators need to approach the experts in related disciplines, such as psychology, education, sociology, technology, medical science, chemistry, physics, statistics, and several others to find out what knowledge from these disciplines could be applied to teaching of a subject. A superficial treatment of important subject matters can then he replaced by an adequate coverage of significant and related disciplines.

The L&IS educational objectives can be classified on the basis of behaviour of students. The abilities and skills, along with the behaviour they lead to as designed by Bloom[2] are:

Intellectual abilities and skills	*Types of behaviour*
1. Comprehensions	To illustrate, to explain, to draw conclusions, to identify, to examine, to comprehend.
2. Application	To apply, to relate, to solve, to select, to use.
3. Analysis	To identify parts of the whole, to express relations between ideas, to analyse elements, relationships and principles for consistency as well as discrepancy.
4. Synthesis	To plan, to create, to design, to service abstract relations.
5. Evaluation	To evaluate, to judge, to appraise, to conclude, to compare.

Finally, it can be said that there can be no development without the necessary modifications in the present curriculum, and implementation of evaluation results makes it possible to bring about these modifications.

2.4. *Need for Curriculum Development in L&IS Education*

The development of curriculum in L&IS education is needed primarily because L&IS as a discipline is still in the process of emerging in India. Several areas of L&IS are yet to be developed. As new knowledge in L&IS grows, new discoveries are made, of known facts are scientifically organized and interpreted, the development of curriculum for L&IS becomes imperative. The emerging discipline of L&IS needs to develop its curriculum because the future development and growth of the discipline will be largely affected by the initial planning of the curriculum.[3]

Another reason for curriculum development in L&IS is the changing of information environment. The curriculum planners have to ascertain what new objectives are to be selected for meeting the emerging needs; what new knowledge could be used to realise these objectives; and what new learning experience could be offered to learners to make education more meaningful to meet the challenges for modern times.[4]

Employment of new persons in the library requires proper training to qualify for jobs. All areas of L&IS need to be enriched through new knowledge and new methods of teaching and training. The curriculum planners must recognise the new subjects and their contents which are to be taught to enable the learner to get the maximum benefit of scientific advancement, modern technology and industrial development. The new role expectations of library personnel demand newer concepts in L&IS education. Therefore, the L&IS curricula need to be recast in the areas of resource development and information environment.

3. **Objectives of BLIS Course**

Any programme of a education must have a set of objectives. The objectives change from time to time to accommodate new developments and aspirations within the field and beyond it. These developments identify new problem areas necessitating the modifications in objectives. Resilience to respond to change is thus essential.

In the Indian context the courses at the BLIS level are expected to provide a balanced and well-rounded training, integrating theory with practicals and covering with equal emphasis on all aspects of professional work. It is also the intention of the library schools that the courses should reflect the present needs of libraries, by offering interesting and useful packages of courses of study. In order to achieve this, it is necessary to take a few steps to restructure the curriculum by enlarging the contents of course by adding papers on Literature Survey in the field of science, social science or humanities and also by combining some of the existing papers, such as Documentation and Reference Work, Organisation and Administration, etc. All this should be carried out without diluting their contents but by increasing the workload of students accordingly. Moreover, the library schools should include some management course after a proper blend of library situations and management techniques. In addition to the above reforms, emphasis should be laid on the field work, so that the students can gain experience in understanding the problems encountered in live situations.[5]

In our present day course, the students should be exposed to new environmental information systems. They should be acquainted with the application of information technology. The library schools, therefore, should be geared to organize such courses.

The curriculum should be tailored particularly for the BLIS students who are going to serve the industry and business houses. They have to face the changing environment. They should be able to adapt themselves to the new environment and feel that they are an integral part of the organization and not a secluded entity.

4. Analysis of Curriculum Design of West Bengal Library Schools

In West Bengal there are five universities (viz., Calcutta, Jadavpur, Burdwan, Rabindra Bharati and Vidyasagar)[6] which are awarding BLS/BLIS degree. Before the work of the analysis, a clear picture of course of study of West Bengal Library Schools in BLS/BLIS level is furnished below:

4.1 *Calcutta University*

Papers included in the B.Lib.Sc. Course of study show that there are 8 papers, each carrying 100 marks. A student is required for passing the examination, a minimum of 30 per cent marks in each theoretical and practical papers, and in aggregate 40 per cent of the full marks of all the papers. The intake is 100, which is divided into two sections, each section containing 50 students. It is an evening course and the classes are normally held from 5 p.m. to 9 p.m. The admission requirements for this level include graduation from any recognised university with good academic background. Selection is made strictly on the basis of merit. Some seats are kept reserved for deputed candidates from different organisations and institutions and candidates from outside West Bengal. The credit of this university lies in opening a separate faculty for library science with a post of separate Dean.

4.2 *Jadavpur University*

The course of study in the degree level is divided into two parts, viz., theoretical and practical papers. Theoretical papers include paper I to V and practical papers certain papers VI to VIII. Each paper comprises 100 marks and thus the total marks for entire course are 800. Again, for each theoretical paper, 20 marks are set apart for sessional tests. The marks in practical papers are covered by sessional tests and assignments. The qualifying marks for passing the examination is a minimum of 30 per cent marks in each theory paper and 40 per cent marks in aggregate. Students are prepared for colloquium, and papers related to Documentation and Colon Classification are taught with special emphasis. The intake is 55. A few seats are reserved for deputed candidates from different institutions.

The university also introduced an evening course in BLIS level with an intake of 40. The duration of the course is 18 months. It is primarily intended for working librarians.

4.3 *Burdwan University*

The BLIS course is divided into 10 papers. Each paper consists of 75 marks. There is a provision for viva-voce in the course of study and 50 marks are allotted for viva-voce. The total marks thus are 800. Again in papers II, V, VI, VII, VIII and in papers IX and X (classification and cataloguing practicals) 15 and 25 marks are set apart respectively for internal assessment. Viva-voce test is conducted on entire course of study. To pass the examination a candidate must obtain a minimum of 40 per cent marks including internal assessment marks in each theory paper and 45 per cent marks including internal assessment marks in each practical paper. The intake of this level is 60. About half of the intake is reserved for deputed candidates from different organisations and institutions.

4.4 *Rabindra Bharati University*

The university started the BLIS course in 1984. It is a part time course and classes are held in the evening. No standard is maintained in regard to the number of students to be admitted in the course. Therefore, the intake ranges from 80 to 100 in each session.

The structure of papers in the course of study has been designed on the pattern of Burdwan University. Even the nomenclature of each paper has got a close affinity with the Burdwan University. But the distribution of marks in each paper is quite different. Ten marks of internal assessment and 15 marks for project work are allotted for paper I to VIII respectively. There are no separate internal assessment marks for paper IX, X, i.e. classification and cataloguing practice, but 25 marks are allotted for project work in these papers. Teachers suggest different assignments/projects work to the students. The topic of these assignments/projects cover the entire aspects of L&IS to be done during the period of study and must be submitted before the commencement of the final examination. To pass the examination a student must secure 35 per cent marks in each paper in the final examination,

45 per cent marks in practicals, project work, viva-voce and internal assessment, and 40 per cent in aggregate.

4.5 *Vidyasagar University*

This is a new university opened by the State Government in 1984 in the Midnapore district under the name of Pandit Iswar Chander Vidyasagar, the greatest social reformer of the 19th century Bengal. The university introduced the BLIS course in 1985 with an intake of 30. The course of study has been drafted in a different line. It has got no similarity with the other library schools of the State.

The syllabus has been split into two parts. Part I contains 'core subjects' consisting of papers I to VI. Among the six papers, papers I to IV are theoretical and papers V to VI are practicals. Each paper in part I comprises 100 marks. Paper VIII is divided into three sections. Section I comprises 50 marks, Section II (special assignments) 30 marks, and section III (viva-voce on the assignment) 20 marks respectively. There are no separate papers for Documentation and Management. Out of three special papers (viz., Academic, Public, and Special libraries) one has to be taken by a student. The pass requirement is a minimum of 30 per cent in each theoretical and practical paper and in aggregate 40 per cent of the total marks of all the papers. In paper VIII of each group, the pass requirement is a minimum of 30 per cent in section I, and 40 per cent in section II and III respectively.

4.6 *Observation*

After careful analysis of the curricula of these universities it is found that no norms and standards are maintained in regard to course content of BLIS level. From the investigation of the course content of BLIS course in West Bengal Library Schools, it is evident that almost all the curricula are unbalanced and unsuitable and do not reflect the present day changing environment of library and information science. In BLIS level all library schools, except Jadavpur and Vidyasagar, recommended separate papers on Library Organization and have a provision for the papers to be studied as a combined paper. Vidyasagar makes a strange provision. The paper 'Library and Society' covers some specified aspects of library organisation and administration. But it omits many important topics such as library legislation, library authority, library finance, library buildings and library activities from the course of study.

Burdwan and Rabindra Bharati divide the paper 'Bibliography into two separate papers: (1) Physical bibliography which is combined with 'Conservation of reading materials' to one full paper; (2) Systematic bibliography which is combined with book selection to make one full paper. On the other hand Calcutta and Jadavpur Universities combine 'Physical Bibliography, and Book Selection' together as one full paper. Vidyasagar makes a combination of 'Bibliography and Reference Service'. It omits Book Selection altogether. As regards Reference service Burdwan and Rabindra Bharati Universities provide for the study of reference service under a single caption 'Reference and Information Work' and list a separate paper on Documentation. Calcutta and Jadavpur both study 'Reference Service and Documentation'. It prescribes optional subjects consisting of three groups' viz., (a) Public library system, (b) Academic library system, and (c) Special libraries and information services. Any one of the groups is to be taken by the student. In BLIS level the provision for specialized study is something exaggerative. Again in some schools papers on 'Systematic Bibliography', 'Documentation', and 'Reference work' are partially practical.

All library schools agree that library classification and library cataloguing should be a separate full paper both in theory and practice. In Library Classification (Theory) all syllabi are quite comprehensive. Jadavpur and Vidyasagar provide for a comparative study of DDC and UDC in library classification (practical). Calcutta has a provision for detailed study of DDC only in practical paper, while Burdwan and Rabindra Bharati provide for the study of both DDC and CC in this paper. In Library Cataloguing (Theory) the curriculum drafted by all the schools are almost identical and prescribed detailed study of the theoretical aspect of the paper. In practical paper all universities make the study of only AACR II, but Burdwan has made a provision for the comparative study of both AACR II and CCC. But the practices followed in regard to the evaluation for classification and cataloguing practicals in both the levels vary widely from school to school. However, it appears that Burdwan provides the most useful course of study for these two practical papers. Thus, it reveals that approximately 50 per cent of the course content in BLIS programmes relates to cataloguing and classification – theory and practice.

There are some papers in BLIS curricula which are vary important from utilitarian point of view. Still, very important facets of management like the personnel, financial and committee management, public relations and the like are dealt with inadequately. Motivating users and educating them in exploiting the library materials and services are the topics conspicuous by their absence in these curricula.

Further, the present survey reveals that there is no uniformity in regard to course content, methods of evaluation, distribution of marks, admission criteria to the courses, class periods, duration of the course etc, in these schools. Lack of a uniform set of norms and standards also prevails in the teaching techniques of various core subjects and even in the distribution of minimum marks in passing the examination. Lack of uniformity also prevails in assessing internal assignments and other project work.

4.7 *Suggestions*

After a close study of syllabi in BLIS level of West Bengal library schools, the following suggestions are made:

(i) There is no scope for revamping the curricula. The aim should be to delete what is repugnant and incorporate what is relevant according to the present day library environment in the country. Of course, this should not be done ignoring the world trends in the field;

(ii) It is not advisable to permeate our syllabi with such a stress on cataloguing and classification techniques. The practice of prenatal cataloguing has also diminished the need for too much stress on these techniques. Therefore, telescoping of cataloguing and classification theory into one paper, and deleting the canons from compulsory papers in theory appears advisable. AACR may be put in one semester and the CCC in other;

(iii) The coordination and cooperation among various schools should be strengthened by exchanging specialists, experienced teachers and faculty members;

(iv) Regular seminars, refresher/orientation courses, summer institutes and specialized courses in L&IS should be organised by the library schools from time to time for the development of the curricula and for updating the knowledge of the working librarians and teachers in library science in view of the rapid advancements in the field of L&IS;

(v) The teacher student ratio recommended by the UGC Review Committee should be maintained to achieve effective and efficient training;

(vi) The existing curricula should be restructured by adjusting the contents of the courses by adding the required new topics, and by removing the outmoded subjects. New subjects, such as Reader's Services, Subject reference materials, Communication media, Automation, Motivation and Education of users, outreach services and a host of other modern sophisticated ideas are yet to be accommodated in our course contents;

(vii) Education tour programme must be compulsory in the curricula for exposure and observation;

(viii) Instead of expansion, we should now turn to consolidation. No school should be allowed to be established without proper standards;

(ix) Accrediting body like the one in our medical profession can only perhaps check proliferation of substandard courses or courses run without necessary infrastructure. Under the Act of 1965, UGC has the responsibility of maintaining standards of teaching and therefore, it can take some measures to prevent proliferation of courses of the above nature; and

(x) A joint committee of the professional associations to review the current state of affairs in L&IS education in the country need to be established.

5. Conclusion

Presently, we are engaged in imparting the knowledge of yesterday to the generation of tomorrow. It is a fact that an exploding change has come in the field of L&IS education system. To cope with this change, restructuring of L&IS curriculum has become indispensable. The curriculum attached to L&IS education lacks proper objectives as well as resilience to accommodate change. It pines in silence for touch of a healing hand. The delay in doing so may not only be dangerous but even disastrous. We have a brave and momentous responsibility to invigorate it and make it responsive to present situations. It needs change, a total change. And, the change is essential in everything, everywhere. It is the breath of life and solitary guarantee for continuance, survival and growth. Let us, therefore, be up doing the change and modernise the pattern of our L&IS education so that it is responsive to the needs of the society of today as well as tomorrow.

REFERENCES

1. Lulla, B.P., Need for better curriculum administration in India, *Journal of Regional College of Education*, Bhopal, 3, 1969, 56-60.
2. Bloom Benjamin (ed.), Taxonomy of educational objectives, *Handbook* 1: Cognitive domain. New York, David McKay, 1965.
3. Tyler, R.W., *Basic Principles of Curriculum and Instruction: Syllabus for Education*, 305, Chicago, University of Chicago Press, 1965.
4. Chandra, A., *Curriculum Development and Evaluation in Education*, New Delhi, Sterling.
5. Patil, P.K., Curriculum design for Master's Degree course in Library and Information Science (Education in Library Science 17) *Library Science with a slant to Documentation*, 15, 3, Sept. 1978, 146-148.
6. Prospectus of Calcutta, Jadavpur, Burdwan, Rabindrabharati, Vidyasagar Universities.

9

RESTRUCTURING THE COURSE CONTENT

P.S.G: KUMAR

1. Framework

The educational framework of library and information science in India at present is as follows:

Course Title	*Sponsor*
1. Certificate	Library associations; colleges affiliated to universities; University departments
2. Diploma	Women's polytechnics; Library associations
3. Degree	University department; colleges affiliated to universities; Open Universities
4. Master's	University departments; Through Correspondence
5. Associateship	Autonomous institutions
6. M.Phil	University departments
7. Ph.D.	University departments
8. Short-term	Libraries; Documentation centres; University departments; Professional associations

2. Course Contents

The courses offered by the schools before 1950, comprehend papers on organisation; administration; classification; cataloguing; bibliography;

reference service; book selection etc. Many schools included a paper on general knowledge. The pattern evolved by Ranganathan wayback in 1930s is still being followed with slight modifications, and in some schools, as it is.

2.1 *Developments in 1950s*

In 1950s, India saw the introduction of documentation techniques with the establishment of INSDOC. Systematic documentation services were started in various ministries and special libraries. Organisation of micro literature demanded depth classification schedules. These concepts gradually found place in the courses of some of the schools in 1950.

2.2 *Changes in 1960s*

Establishment of DRTC; starting of Associateship by INSDOC and M.Lib.Sc. by few universities brought in change in the course contents. Subjects such as indexing and abstracting, reprography and micrography; designing of depth classification schedules, documentation lists etc were incorporated.

2.3 *New Thrusts in 1970s*

Use of computers in library and bibliographic information handling had started in 1950s and became common in 1960s. But, its impact on library and information curriculum was felt in 1970s. New management principles and techniques also made an impact on L&IS. These resulted in the introduction of subjects such as computer based library and information systems, management principles and techniques; systems analysis; statistical methods; user education; construction and use of thesaurus etc.

2.4 *Trends in 1980s*

The impact of 'new technology' has been phenomenal in 1980s. Communication technology; bibliographic databases, data banks and printing; on-line retrieval; technical writing, editing and printing; marketing of information etc, are demanding a place in the curriculum.

Before 1950

Administration; Organisation; Classification; Cataloguing; Bibliography; Book selection; Reference service.

1950s

Documentation; Sociology of Librarianship; Universe of Knowledge; Depth classification.

1960s

Designing of depth classification schedules; Repro-micrographies; Abstracting and indexing; Translation service; Documentation list.

1970s

Computer based information systems; Management principles; statistical methods; User education and user studies; Thesaurus in information retrieval; Bibliometrics.

1980s

Databases and data services; Micro computers and CD-ROMs; Communication technologies and information networks; on-line retrieval; Technical writing and reporting etc.

3. **Structure**

Messrs S.P. Agrawal and Manohar Lal[1] identified the following scheme of papers at various levels.

3.1 *Certificate Course*

(1) Library management (Routine operations)
(2) Library organisation
(3) Library classification (Theory and Practice)
(5) Bibliography and Reference Service

3.2 *Diploma Course (of Women's Polytechnics)*

(1) Library and society
(2) Bibliography
(3) Classification
(4) Cataloguing
(5) Library administration
(6) Library correspondence
(7) Reference service

3.3 *Degree Courses*

(1) Library administration
(2) Library organisation
(3) Physical bibliography and reference service
(4) Classification (Theory and Practice)
(5) Cataloguing (Theory and Practice)
(6) Documentation

3.4 *Master's Course*

(1) Universe of knowledge (its development and structure)
(2) Depth classification (theory)
(3) Advanced cataloguing
(4) Library systems
(5) Literature survey
(6) Research methodology
(7) Information systems
(8) Project report

3.5 *Associateship Course*

(1) Information sources
(2) Information processing and organisation
(3) Information and communication
(4) Information systems management
(5) Information technology
(6) Research methodology
(7) Project report

The above description gives a generalised structure of papers of various courses. However, it is to be noted that there are certain deviations to this. The above study reveals that, by and large, the syllabi of various schools remained unchanged, inspite of drastic changes and rapid developments in the field of library and information science and service.

4. Restructuring of Course

4.1 *General Guidelines*

The New Education Policy, 1986 has laid down general guidelines for restructuring of courses.[2] The restructured courses should comprehend:

(1) Foundation courses;
(2) Core courses;
(3) Applied courses;
(4) Work experience; and
(5) Professional development

The Foundation Courses should aim at creating awareness of areas such as history and development of libraries; library and society; philosophical and sociological foundations of librarianship etc.

Core courses should provide broad familiarity with basic components of the discipline. In L&IS, these include management; technical processing; bibliography and reference; documentation and information service.

Applied courses aim at application of theoretical knowledge in relevant areas and impart practical skills and techniques required in application. In our discipline these include classification and cataloguing practice; compilation of bibliographies; preparation of documentation lists; user education; fact finding; and reference service.

Work experience is a programme that related theoretical knowledge to practical field and productivity. In L&IS education work experience can be provided by.

(1) Pre course apprenticeship
(2) Post course internship
(3) Parallel work experience
(4) Educational tours and visits; and
(5) Project work

Professional development accounts for professionalism by way of: (1) General education; (2) Professional education; and (3) Professional training as well as personality development through the knowledge of (a) literature and languages; (b) human psychology and understanding of user needs; and ethical and moral responsibility of the profession. L&IS curriculum should provide basic knowledge and understanding of these values.

5. Curriculum

It is not desirable to prescribe uniform syllabi for various L&IS courses run in the country. However, a set of core and optional papers can be listed here. The individual school will have freedom to choose.

5.1 *CLSC*

At CLSC level there be five theory and one or two practical papers.

(1) Library administration and organisation
(2) Classification (Theory)
(3) Cataloguing (Theory)
(4) Bibliography and book selection
(5) Reference sources and service
(6) Practical test in classification and cataloguing

5.2 *BLISc*

(1) *Foundation course*
Library and society

(2) *Core courses*
1. Library organisation and management
2. Library classification
3. Library cataloguing
4. Documentation
5. Reference sources and services

(3) *Auxiliary courses*
1. Bibliography
2. Book selection

(4) *Applied courses*

1. Classification practice
2. Cataloguing practice
3. Bibliography/Bibliographic essay
4. Library records
5. Evaluation of reference sources
6. Fact finding
7. Book selection

(5) *Optionals/Electives*

1. Information science
2. Subject indexing / Indexing theory
3. Computer applications

(6) *Work experience*

1. Educational tour
2. Internship

5.3 *MLISc*

(1) *Foundation courses*

1. Universe of knowledge
2. Research methodology
3. Statistical methods
4. Systems analysis
5. Comparative librarianship
6. Management techniques
7. Operations research
8. Linguistics
9. Behavioural science
10. Communication theory

(2) *Core courses*

1. Classification, Advanced/Depth
2. Cataloguing, Advanced
3. Information science and technology
4. Information systems and programmes

(3) *Applied courses*

1. Classification, Advanced /depth (practical)
2. Cataloguing, Advanced (practical)

(4) *Optionals/Electives*

1. Information and literature sources in (a) Humanities; (b) Social sciences; (c) Sciences; (d) Medical sciences; (e) Engineering and technology; (f) Agricultural sciences etc.
2. Computer applications
3. L&IS education
4. Library systems (a) Public; (b) Academic; (c) Research and technical; (d) Agricultural; (e) Medical; (f) Engineering and technology; (g) Medical etc.
5. Bibliographical control
6. Work experience 1. Seminar; 2. Project

5.4 *M.Phil*

(1) *Foundation course*

1. Research Methods

(2) *Core courses*

1. Library planning and management

(3) *Optionals*

1. University and college library system
2. Research and technical library system
3. Public library system
4. Information processing and organisation
5. Information transfer and dissemination
6. Comparative librarianship
7. Education for Library and Information Science

(4) *Work experience*

1. Dissertation

6. Conclusion

The above listing is only illustrative. Each library school should see that all the types of courses form part of the curriculum. Selection of specific courses under each type should be based on loud thinking on the following points: (1) Level of the course; (2) Duration; (3) Teaching staff; (4) Physical facilities; (5) Cooperation of libraries; (6) General background of the students; (7) Job market; (8) Manpower needs; and (9) Programme goals.

REFERENCES

1 Agrawal, S.P. and Manohar Lal, Library and information science education in India: Achievements and perspectives. (In Kumar (PSG). *Norms, Guidelines and Standards for Library and its Future*. Paper BA).

2 Kumar, P.S.G., Norms, guidelines and standards for library and information science education: working document. ILA, CSC on LIS, 1989.

10

RESTRUCTURING OF SYLLABUS FOR SEMESTER SYSTEM : A Case Study of BLIS and MLIS Course of Vikram University

S.S. AGRAWAL and SUDHIR KUMAR

Introduction

Semester means a period of term of six months, the college half year (Shorter Oxford English Dictionary). It is clear that the semester system signifies the division of academic year into two parts. It also implies that courses are designed to cover one semester (instead of a year), that final examinations are to be held twice a year.

The quantities of contents in various subjects would be proportionate to two semesters. Framing of syllabus for semester system is not done simply by breaking the old traditional syllabus into two halves. The areas like contents and abilities have to be taken into consideration. The areas for earlier semester have to be of lower order involving information. Complex areas may be included for the later semester. The problem areas must deal with simpler abilities like comprehension of knowledge, while later on abilities such as analysis, synthesis, application, etc. may be included. By and large there must be a built-in continuity in respect of both contents and abilities. The structure of the whole course is to be designed in such a way that it moves from simplex to complex.

The problem of designing semester course for BLIS is much more difficult since the entrants are unfamiliar with the basic knowledge of the subject. In case of traditional examination system, the logical sequence of simple to complex areas does not pose much problem. But this is more important in semester system. The sequence of papers and units in each paper should be logical and helpful. It is a difficult task to design syllabus for BLIS and MLIS courses.

2. Semester System at Vikram University

The act to establish Vikram University as federal university came into force in 1957, soon after the formation of Madhya Pradesh by the States Reorganisation Commission, 1956. Previously this area was under the jurisdiction of Agra University, Agra.

The Department of Library Science is the first department of this university. In the beginning it had Certificate and Diploma courses in Library Science. In 1963 the nomenclature of Diploma Course was changed to Degree as Bachelor of Library Science. The Certificate course was discontinued. In 1971 it started MLS, the first in M.P. Now the Department is changed to School of Studies in Library and Information Science, imparting courses for BLIS and MLIS. It is also proposed to start M. Phil in L&IS from 1990 July, the first in Madhya Pradesh.

This year the university decided to adopt semester system in all the post-graduate subjects being taught in all the university teaching departments in all faculties. This decision came very late and it became very difficult to give enough time to the structure of syllabus. Previously the semester system was introduced in only Science Faculties of the University Departments, but was discontinued a few years back. The courses in affiliated colleges are on old pattern and the semester system has not been introduced there.

School of Studies in Library and Information Science of the University also suitably modified the syllabus on the basis of general guidelines of the University, and considering some basic facts of the course and availability of resource and staff.

3. General Guidelines – Basic Facts

The following basic facts are worth observing:

(1) Each paper in Previous and Final will be divided equally.
(2) Each paper will be taught in both the semesters.
(3) Each paper will be examined in both the semesters dividing the maximum marks into exactly half for each semester.
(4) There will be continuous internal assessment of 20 per cent

marks in each paper.

(5) The work load of the teachers will be decided as per the UGC guidelines.

(6) MLIS and BLIS will have only two semesters each.

(7) There are at present four teachers in L&IS – one Professor, two readers, and one lecturer. As far as possible all the four teachers will take one lecture everyday in both the semesters.

(8) New posts of two lecturers are likely to be filled up by the beginning of the next session (now filled up).

(9) M.Phil in L&IS may start from 1990-91.

4. Stage One : Splitting Each Paper into two Halves

As per university guidelines, all the papers were split into two halves. The course contents of the syllabus was divided logically. It was decided to retain 8 papers in BLIS and 7 papers in MLIS in each semester. Each examination paper will be of 40 marks and 10 marks will be allotted for internal assessment. The papers and the scheme of examination is as follows:

Bachelor of Library and Information Science

Paper	Subject	Internal assessment	Exams. Marks	Duration	Total Marks
1	2	3	4	5	6
First Semester					
I	Lib Cln-Th	10	40	2 hours	50
II	Lib Cln-Pr	10	40	2 hours	50
III	Lib Catg-Th	10	40	2 hours	50
IV	Lib Catg-Pr	10	40	2 hours	50
V	Ref Ser & Ref Sources	10	40	2 hours	50
VI	Docn & Inf Ser	10	40	2 hours	50
VII	Lib Orgn	10	40	2 hours	50
VIII	Lib Admn	10	40	2 hours	50
		80	320		400
Second Semester					
IX	Lib Cln-Th	10	40	2 hours	50
X	Lib Cln-Pr	10	40	2 hours	50
XI	Lib Catg-Th	10	40	2 hours	50
XII	Lib Catg-Pr	10	40	2 hours	50
XIII	Ref Ser & Ref Sources	10	40	2 hours	50
XIV	Docn & Inf Ser	10	40	2 hours	50
XV	Lib Orgn	10	40	2 hours	50
XVI	Lib Admn	10	40	2 hours	50
	Grand Total	160	640		800

Master of Library and Information Science

Papers

1	2	3	4	5	6
First Semester					
I	Uni Know	10	40	2 hours	50
II	Adv Lib Cln-Th	10	40	2 hours	50
III	Adv Lib Cln-Pr	10	40	2 hours	50
IV	Adv Lib Catg-Th	10	40	2 hours	50
V	Adv Lib Catg-Pr	10	40	2 hours	50
VI	Inf Sys & Programmes	10	40	2 hours	50
VII	Inf Stor & Retrieval (Optional)	10	40	2 hours	50
		70	280		350
Second Semester					
VIII	Univ Know	10	40	2 hours	50
IX	Adv Lib Cln-Th	10	40	2 hours	50
X	Adv Lib Cln-Pr	10	40	2 hours	50
XI	Adv Lib Catg-Th	10	40	2 hours	50
XII	Adv Lib Catg-Pr	10	40	2 hours	50
XIII	Inf Sys & Programmes	10	40	2 hours	50
XIV	Inf Stor & Ret (opt)	10	40	2 hours	50
XV	Project/Dissertation	-	100		100
	Grand Total	140	660		800

On critical evaluation of the system, it was felt that it will not be practical to hold examination for eight papers at the end of each semester. There may be overlapping of units in the examination. Unlike M.A/M.Sc, BLIS and MLIS are one year courses, and traditionally have eight papers in one year. There are only four papers in previous and Final in other courses. The procedure of splitting each paper into two halves may be practicable for these courses. But in BLIS and MLIS it was found to be unpracticable.

5. Stage Two: Splitting of Courses into Halves

Due to the above difficulties, the Board of Studies decided to divide the course into two halves instead of dividing each paper into two halves. Thus there are only four papers in one semester in BLIS and MLIS. This is also helpful since the units of each paper were not to be divided.

But there are various alternatives possible in the splitting of whole course into two halves. Each may have its own merits and demerits which are yet to be tested and decided. There are merits and demerits of each alternative, depending on local conditions and facilities available. The various papers are named A to H in BLIS and MLIS, and are as follows:

Paper	*BLIS*	*MLIS*
(A)	Lib Classn (Th)	Library Classn (Th)
(B)	Lib Classn (Pr)	Library Classn (Pr)
(C)	Lib Catg (Th)	Library Cg (Th)
(D)	Lib Catg (Pr)	Library Catg (Pr)
(E)	Ref Service	Universe of Knowledge
(F)	Docn & Inf Science	Information Systems
(G)	Library Organisation	Information Retrieval (opt)
(H)	Lib Administration	Dissertation/Project

On discussing the various problems and facilities available it was decided to adopt model 5 – Theory first – Practical later. There are more holidays in the first half of the session. So there are less number of working days in the first semester. This factor was given considerable thought and it was decided that it will not be practicable to complete classification and cataloguing practicals in the first semester. Though, practically it is difficult to give theory first without the knowledge of practicals. For this basic knowledge of practicals was given which will reduce work load in the second semester. The model was found suitable, though it may not be helpful in all situations. The scheme of examination for BLIS and MLIS for both the semesters is as follows:

VARIOUS MODELS

Model 1 : Theoretical Papers First

Semester	BLIS	MLIS
	1 -G-Lib Orgn	1 -A- Lib Cln-Th
	2 -H-Lib Admn	2 -B- Lib Cln-Pr
(I)	3 -E-Ref Service	3 -C- Lib Catg-Th
	4 -F-Doc Inf Science	4 -D- Lib Catg-Pr

	5	-A-Lib Cln-Th	5 -E-	UK
(II)	6	-B-Lib Cln-Pr	6 -F-	Inf systems
	7	-C-Lib Catg-Th	7 -G-	Inf Retrieval
	8	-D-Lib Catg-Pr	8 -H-	Dissertation/Project

Model II : Theory and Practical Together

	1	-A-Lib Cln-Th	1 -E-	UK
(I)	2	-B-Lib Cln-Pr	2 -F-	Inf Systems
	3	-C-Lib Catg-Th	3 -G-	Inf Ret (Optional)
	4	-D-Lib Catg-Pr	4 -H-	Dissn/Project
	5	-G-Lib Orgn	5 -A-	Lib Cln-Th
(II)	6	-H-Lib Admn	6 -B-	Lib Cln-Pr
	7	-E-Ref Service	7 -C-	Lib Catg-Th
	8	-F-Doc Inf Service	8 -D-	Lib Catg-Pr

Model III : Only One Practical in One Semester

	1	-A-Lib Cln-Th	1 -C-	Lib Catg-Th
	2	-B-Lib Cln-Pr	2 -D-	Lib Catg-Pr
(I)	3	-G-Lib Orgn	3 -E-	UK
	4	-H-Lib Admn	4 -F-	Inf systems
	5	-C-Lib Catg-Th	5 -A-	Lib Cln-Th
(II)	6	-D-Lib Catg-Pr	6 -B-	Lib Cln-Pr
	7	-E-Ref Service	7 -G-	Inf Retrieval (Optional)
	8	-F-Doc Inf Science	8 -H-	Dissn/Project

Model IV : Both Practicals in First Semester

	1	-A-Lib Cln-pr	1 -B-	Lib Cln-Pr
(I)	2	-C-Lib Catg-Pr	2 -D-	Lib Catg-Pr
	3	-G-Lib Orgn	3 -E-	UK
	4	-H-Lib Admn	4 -G-	Inf Ret (Optional)
	5	-B-Lib Cln-Th	5 -A-	Lib Cln Th
(II)	6	-D-Lib Catg-Th	6 -C-	Lib Catg-Th
	7	-E-Inf Ser	7 -F-	Inf Sys
	8	-F-Doc Inf Sc	8 -G-	Dissn/Project

Model V : Only Theory in First Semester

	1	-A-Lib Cln-Th	1 -A-	Lib Cln-Th
(I)	2	-C-Lib Catg-Th	2 -C-	Lib Catg-Th
	3	-E-Ref Service	3 -E-	UK
	4	-G-Lib Orgn	4 -H-	Inf Systems

	5 -B-Lib Cln-Th		5 -B- Lib Cln-Pr
(II)	6 -D-Lib Catg-Pr		6 -D- Lib Catg-Pr
	7 -F-Doc Inf Service		7 -G- Inf Ret (Optional)
	8 -H-Lib Admn		8 -H- Dissn/Project

SCHEME OF PAPERS FOR THE SEMESTER SYSTEM

(A) B.LIB. & INF. SC

First Semester

	Internal assessment	Exams. Marks Univ.	Duration	Total Marks
1. Lib Cln-Th-P-I	20	80	3 hours	100
2. Lib Catg-Th-P-II	20	80	3 hours	100
3. Ref Ser & Ref Sou-P-III	20	80	3 hours	100
4. Lib Orgn-P-IV	20	80	3 hours	100
	80	320		400
Second Semester				
5. Lib Cln-Pr-P-V	20	80	3 hours	100
6. Lib Catg-Pr-P-VI	20	80	3 hours	100
7. Doc & Inf Ser-P-VII	20	80	3 hours	100
8. Lib Admn-P-VIII	20	80	3 hours	100
Grand Total	160	640		800

(B) M.LIB. & INF. SC.

First Semester	1	2	3	4
1. Uni Know P-I	20	80	3 hours	100
2. Adv Lib Cln-Th-P-II	20	80	3 hours	100
3. Adv Lib Catg-Th-P-III	20	80	3 hours	100
4. Inf Sys & Prog-P-IV	20	80	3 hours	100
	80	320		400
Second Semester				
5. Adv Lib Cln-Pr-P-V	20	80	3 hours	100
6. Adv Lib Catg-Pr-P-VI	20	80	3 hours	100
7. Inf Stor & Ret-Opt-P-VII	20	80	3 hours	100
8. Project/Dissn P-VIII	—	—		100
Grand Total	140	560		800

(C) M.PHIL

First Semester	1	2	3	4
1. Res Methods	20	80	3 hours	100
2. Lib Planning & Management	20	80	3 hours	100
3 Any One of the Following Options :				
(a) Univ & Coll Lib System	20	80	3 hours	100
(b) Rs & Tech Lib System	20	80	3 hours	100
(c) Pub Lib System	20	80	3 hours	100
(d) Inf Processing & Orgn	20	80	3 hours	100
(e) Inf Transfer & Dissemination	20	80	3 hours	100
(f) Comparative Librarianship	20	80	3 hours	100
(g) Edun for Lib & Inf Sc	20	80	3 hours	100
Second Semester				
IV Dissertation	-	-	- (out of which 50 marks will be for Viva-Voce)	100

6. Basic Rules

1. The Course for BLIS and MLIS shall be divided in the semesters covering one academic session. The first semester shall comprise four papers, and the second semester shall also comprise four papers.
2. The examination for the first semester shall normally be conducted in November/December, and for the second semester in April/May of each year.
3. Each semester examination shall be by means of theory papers, practicals if any, and internal assessment. There shall be three tests for internal assessment for each paper. The average marks of the best of two tests shall be taken into consideration.
4. A weightage of 80 per cent marks shall be for theory and 20 per cent for internal assessment. Marks on account of internal assessment will be assigned by the concerned teachers of the School of Studies. The Head of the School of Studies will send the internal assessment marks to the university at the end of each semester.
5. If a candidate fails to obtain 40 per cent marks in BLIS and 50

per cent in MLIS in the internal assessment of any paper separately, he/she shall not be permitted to appear in the examination of the semester.

6. The minimum passing marks will be 40 per cent in BLIS and 50 per cent in MILS in aggregate in each semester examination.
7. If a candidate fails in any one or more papers of any semester examination, he/she will be admitted to the next semester course, and will have to appear as an ex-student in all the papers in the same concerned semester, i.e. the candidate who fails in the first semester of subsequent session. Similarly, if a candidate fails in second semester, he/she will have to appear in the second semester of the subsequent session.
8. If a candidate fails in the internal assessment he/she will be allowed to take admission and attend classes and appear in tests and examination of the concerned semester of the subsequent session only. Such admissions will be in excess to the normal admission quota in the School of Studies.
9. If a candidate fails in both the semester examinations, he/she will be eligible to appear as an ex-student provided he/she has passed the internal assessment examination. Such a chance will be given only once.
10. The fee for each semester examination will be the same as for annual examination.
11. Minimum marks to secure a place in the first division will be 60 per cent in the second division 50 per cent. There will be no third division in M Lib Inf Sc. In BLIS, however, the Third division will be awarded to the students with minimum 40 per cent aggregate marks.

7. Conclusion

The restructuring of syllabus for BLIS and MLIS course is not a simple dictionary of course contents and papers. It has to be logical as well as helpful in a teaching/learning system. A careful examination of contents and paper sequence has to be made. The contents of each paper should be more specific and detailed for the periodic evaluation in a semester system. Contents of the papers are not discussed in this paper and may be included accordingly.

11

INTEGRATED MLIS PROGRAMME : A Proposal

K. SIVAREDDY and R.S.R. VARALAKSHMI

1. Introduction

The ALA Council, in 1970, adopted the definition of professional as "the title 'librarian' carries with it the connotation 'professional' in the sense that professional tasks are those which require special background and education on the basis of which library needs are identified. Problems are analysed, goals are set and original and creative solutions are formulated for them, integrating theory into practice and planning, organising, communicating and administering successful programmes of service to users of the library's materials and services".[1]

The definition outlines the competencies required by a professional as a manager. However, the conception and scope of librarianship changed and widened since the time of the above definition. The contemporary librarianship is confronted with information technologies. Information Technology is concerned with the design, installation and operation of information system. To met the challenges of 'Electronic Age' the profession ought to possess more technical competencies. According to Neelameghan, "Students of L&IS may subsequently have different kinds of responsibilities as professionals in relation to on-line searching".[2]

Further, an innovative trend demands that "we must shift the focus of our professional concern away from the library as an institution and towards the skilled professionals" who will become a professional 'practitioner' on par with medical and legal practitioners".[3]

To cope with the new trends, the schools of Library and Information Science are given the responsibility to train a new breed of professionals who can fit into the present situation. Hence there is a need for a shift in emphasis in L&IS education as per the changes in information environment. There are two alternatives to meet the demand: First is the establishment of Information Technology (IT) as a separate curricular programme at post-graduate level; and the second is to construct a two-year integrated Master degree programme embodying IT.

2. Aim

This paper proposes a plan for a coherent and integrated L&IS curricular programme extending over two years at Master's degree level. It also highlights the role of 'practicum' in coordinating theory and practice.

3. Integrated Programme of L&IS Education

The field of information science is an interdisciplinary area of study. Such a profession must teach the techniques, the body of accepted knowledge, the philosophy behind the practice. It is difficult to teach and learn such a course with limited time schedule of one year BLISc level and one year MLISc level. The rationale of an integrated course is that exposure in the early stages to the basic subjects helps the student have a greater indepth study at the latter stage of the course. Moreover, overlapping can be avoided. Integrated course structure is suitable only when it is not overloaded. Hence pruning of existing course contents of less relevance is necessary to provide the student with sufficient indepth knowledge. The present need is for a featured professional than for a half-baked universal specialist.

The General Information Programme and UNISIST of UNESCO had developed a "Modular Curriculum in Information Studies" under a contract between UNESCO and IFLA, from which curricula can be constructed by individual schools for information studies to meet local needs and circumstances.[4] The proposed programme that follows is based on the structure of modules discussed in the document. The course structure is outlined keeping in view the availability of resources and local needs of India.

In India, librarianship has not attained a stage of sophistication as in the west. The school, junior college, degree college, and university libraries are managing with traditional methods of handling routines. These libraries are slowly adopting to computerisation. On the other hand many of the special libraries had adopted automated house keeping methods. Hence the structure of L&IS curricular programme should be a blend of traditional as well as unconventional skills as one cannot forecast the placement chances of a student.

4. Course Structure

During the first year of the course the student need to know enough of the core ideas and principles of L&IS through basic subjects. Following is the proposed core syllabus for the first year course:

First Year of Integrated L&IS Education Programme

Modules: (Each module of 120 hours duration)

1.	Information in its social and communication context	2 credits
2.	Management of Information System	do
3.	Information Storage and Retrieval - I (Classification	do
4.	Information Storage and Retrieval - II (Cataloguing)	do
5.	Application of information technologies - I	do
6.	Information source	do
7.	Information services and systems	do
8.	Records and viva voce	do
9.	Practicals (Total 120 hours programme): 60 hours in a well-equipped library, 60 hours practical exposure to computer	
		18 credits

The Second year programme is intended to provide an indepth study at an advanced level. The aim is to prepare students with competencies and leadership qualities.

Second Year of Integrated L&IS Education Programme

Modules: (Each module of 180 hours)

1.	Information Storage and Retrieval - III	3 credits
2.	Application of Information Technologies - II	do
3.	Networking and marketing of Information Services	do
4.	Electives: (any one of the modules)	
	(a) Academic information system	3 credits
	(b Community information system	do
	(c) Government information system	do
	(d) Industrial and business information system	do

(e) Health science information system — do
(f) Agricultural Information System — do

5. Practicals (Total 180 hours programme) — do
   90 hours in a related library of specialization
   90 hours practical use of computerised packages and hands on use of retrieval systems.
6. Trend report and viva-voce — do

18 credits

Credit is a measurement of module that indicates relative time allocated for each module. Fifty marks may be allocated for each credit for the evaluation purpose.

As indicated, the proposed integrated course programme treats 'practicum' on par with other modules. Descriptive knowledge is not sufficient unless it is invigorated with practical know-how. In any profession, may be medical, legal or librarianship, a pre-requisite is personal interaction with the real situation and communication with clients. Hence the curricular programmes have to embody practicals along with theoretical insights.

5. Conclusion

The decades ahead offer promise of more change for both library education and librarianship. The traditional one-year BLISc and one-year MLISc programme cannot provide the specialized preparation required for a professional in the current 'information environment'. Library education must respond to these challenges and restructure the curricular programme.

REFERENCES

1. Quoted in Robert, J. Grover, Library and Information education for the learning society — a model curriculum. *Journal of Education for Librarianship and Information Science*, V. 26, No 1, January 1985, p 33.
2. Neelameghan, A., Training in computer applications and on-line search for students of library science — a case study. *Unesco Journal of Information Science, Librarianship and Archives Administration*, V. 5, No 1, 1983 , p 2.
3. Lancaster, F.W., Future librarianship: Preparing for an unconventional career, *Wilson Library Bulletin*, May 1983, p 747.
4. Large, J.A., A modular curriculum in information studies, Paris, Unesco, 1987.

12

LIBRARY AND INFORMATION SCIENCE EDUCATION OF MASTER'S LEVEL IN WEST BENGAL: An Analysis of their Curricula, Design and Structural Differences

P. BARUA

1. Introduction

The history of L&IS education started in India for the first time with the introduction of a library school at Baroda in 1911 by Mr Bordon. Asa Don Dickenson, the librarian of Punjab University also organised a library science training course of three months duration in 1915. The Madras Library Association started a summer school for college librarians in 1929. Later on Madras University started a diploma course (first full time pioneering programme in the country) under the leadership of Ranganathan. The Hooghly District Library Association (HDLA) organised an experimental librarianship camp training centre at Bansberia in association with the Bengal Library Association (BLA) in West Bengal in 1934 and subsequently arranged a regular training course in certificate of librarianship in 1937. In 1935, the Imperial Library (now the National Library of India) also conducted a training course leading to a diploma in librarianship under the supervision of the then librarian Mr K.M. Asadullah. The training programme was continued till 1944, when the Calcutta University introduced a regular diploma course in 1945. Since then a large number of universities in the country and library associations in different states have come forward to introduce the varieties of courses at different levels. At present more than 90 universities impart L&IS education at degree level, and more than 40 universities leading to master's level, and 30 universities provide research facilities leading to a Ph.D degree. Moreover, all state library associations are also providing facilities for training in L&IS at undergraduate level. West Bengal is no exception in this regard and made mighty strides in this direction.

2. L&IS Education in West Bengal

West Bengal has a glorious past in the field of education especially in the field of library development. The library movement which started during the freedom struggle laid foundations not only for the development of different kinds of libraries, but also for the development of library science education in the state. Before and after independence, BLA, National Library of India and Calcutta University were the institutions mainly responsible for the development of L&IS education in West Bengal. At present amongst the nine universities in the State, five (viz, Calcutta, Jadavpur, Burdwan, Rabindra Bharti and Vidyasagar) universities offer L&IS course at post-graduate level, and are awarding B. Lib Sc/BLIS degree. Again four universities viz., Calcutta, Burdwan, Jadavpur, and Vidyasagar have introduced Master degree programme. Calcutta, Burdwan and Jadavpur also offer Ph.D programme leading to a doctoral degree. Kalyani and North Bengal have already decided to introduce the BLIS course in near future. The state library association and some other institutions are providing training facilities leading to a certificate in library science recognised by the state government. In addition to universities and BLA, Institute of Librarians (IOL) are also conducting one-year diploma course in special librarianship and documentation, but the training programme has not been duly recognised by the appropriate authority.

3. Levels of L&IS Courses

The levels of L&IS courses existing at present are as follows:

Certificate level; B Lib Sc level; M Lib Sc level and Ph.D level.

The certificate course is conducted by the BLA and other sponsored institutions with a duration of three to six months. The B Lib Sc or BLSc course is the first degree course of one-year offered by the universities. The M Lib Sc or MLIS course is of usually one full academic year duration in all universities except Calcutta University, where the course is of two years' duration. In addition to Master's course, Burdwan, Calcutta, and Jadavpur Universities also conduct Ph.D programme. It may be mentioned that among these universities Burdwan has already awarded three Ph.D degrees in L&IS from 1984 to 1989.

4. M Lib Sc/MLIS Course in West Bengal

4.1 *Calcutta University*

The Calcutta University introduced a two-year master' degree course in library science in 1974 for the first time in the country. In the beginning the intake was 10 only, which has been increased to 15 from the current session. The minimum requirement for admission to this course is graduation having a diploma or degree in library science from a university recognised by the Calcutta University. Normally fresh candidates having good academic background are admitted to the course on the basis of merit. Two seats are reserved for the employees of the Calcutta University group of libraries deputed by the Registrar. Some of the candidates are also sponsored by the Middle East and African countries, Nepal and Sri Lanka for admission in this course.

4.2 *Burdwan University*

Burdwan University started one-year Master degree course in 1979 with an intake of 8 students and gradually the intake has been increased to 15. The eligibility for admission to the course is First class in B LIb or BLIS with sound academic background for fresh candidates of this university, and graduate having BLIS with considerable years of professional experience for deputed candidates. Admission is granted to a candidate strictly on the basis of merit.

The break-up of the total seats are as follows:

Freshers	10 (Humanities 5, Science 5)
Deputed	3
SC/ST	1
Other 'Versities	1
Total	15

4.3 *Jadavpur University*

Jadavpur University started offering Master's degree course in L&IS from 1984. The duration of the course is one full academic year. The total seats in the beginning were 10. It has now been extended to 15 to 18. The minimum qualification for admission to the course prescribed by the university is graduation with BLIS/Diploma in Library Science from any recognised university with at least three years continuous experience in an established library/documentation/information centre as a full time employee. At the initial stage there was no provision for admission of fresh candidates, but recently three seats are kept reserved for fresh candidates with good academic background.

4.4 *Vidyasagar University*

Vidyasagar University introduced MLIS course in 1987 with an intake capacity of 10 students. Minimum requirement for granting admission into this course is graduation from any recognised university with BLIS degree of this university. Working librarians with considerable years of professional experience are also admitted on merit basis.

5. **Purpose of the Analysis**

All the universities, except the Calcutta University, have adopted the model syllabus with some modifications, recommended by the Review Committee appointed by the UGC under the able stewardship of Ranganathan in 1965. The purpose of this study is to show how far the present syllabi followed in the MLIS programmes conform with the model syllabus of 1965 and draft syllabus circulated by the UGC panel on L&IS in 1982. The analysis clearly testifies that there is a striking uniformity in designing the course module in two universities, viz., Burdwan and Jadavpur with regards to the title of the papers as suggested by the UGC Review Committee. But the syllabi of Calcutta and Vidyasagar Universities have been drawn in different lines. They differ not only in designating the paper, but also in the contents of the papers. However, the outline of the syllabus containing the scheme of papers of L&IS schools in West Bengal is given below.

6. Course Contents of MLIS

6.1 *Calcutta University*

Paper	Title of the paper	Exam. marks	Internal assessment	Duration of exam.
I.	Classification (Th)	80	20	4 hours
II.	Cataloguing (Th)	80	20	4 hours
III.	Bibliography	80	20	4 hours
IV.	Reference Service	80	20	4 hours
V.	Documentation and Inf. Retrieval	80	20	4 hours
VI.	Library planning and architecture	80	20	4 hours
VII.	Book: Its history etc	80	20	4 hours
VIII.	Part 1: Literature of Humanities	40	10	
	Part 2: Literature of Sc & Technology	40	10	4 hours
IX.	Elective papers: Any one of the following			
	(a) Public lib system	80	20	4 hours
	(b) Academic lib system			
	(c) Research and special libraries			
	(d) Lib service for children			
	(e) Manuscript & Archival libraries			
X.	Practical:			
	Part 1: Classification	50		
	Part 2: Cataloguing	50		

The structure of papers shows that there are 10 papers in M Lib Sc course. Each paper consists of 100 marks and the total marks prescribed for the course are 1000. In papers I to IX, 20 marks are set apart for sessional work. Paper VIII and paper IX have been split up into two parts. The two parts in paper X comprise both Classification and Cataloguing practicals. No sessional or internal assessment marks have been assigned for this paper. A student must secure a minimum of 30 per cent marks in each of the theoretical papers and 40 per cent marks in the sessional works of each paper, and a minimum of 50 per cent marks in each of the two parts of the practicals to pass the examination. The minimum marks recommended for Second Class are 50 per cent of the total marks, i.e. 500 and the minimum marks prescribed for First Class are 66 per cent of the full marks i.e. 660

6.2 *Burdwan University*

Paper	Title of the paper	Exam. marks	Internal assessment	Duration of exam.
I.	Universe of subjects and Research Methodology	80	20	4 hrs
II.	Library Management Systems Analysis	80	20	4 hrs
III.	Group A: Advanced classn (Theory)	40	10	2 hrs
	Group B: Advanced cataloguing (Th)	40	10	2 hrs
IV.	Group A: Advanced classn (Pract)	40	10	2 hrs
	Group B: Advanced cataloguing (Pr)	40	10	2 hrs
V.	Information Science & Sources	80	20	4 hrs
VI.	Information Storage & Retrieval	80	20	4 hrs
VII.	Special papers: (Any one of following)	80	20	4 hrs
	(a) Public library system			
	(b) Research & Technical Lib System			
	(c) Academic library system			
	(d) Manuscript & Archival libraries			
VIII.	Dissertation (including 230 marks for viva-voce)	80		

The course module is divided into 8 papers, each paper consisting of 100 marks and the total marks recommended are 800. Among the papers, paper III and IV have been split up into two groups comprising theoretical and practical. Similarly the marks both for examination and internal assessment have been distributed equally in both the groups. Paper VIII for Dissertation is considered as practical and no formal class is held on this paper. Twenty marks are assigned in papers I to VII for internal assessment and 20 marks in paper VIII for viva-voce on the dissertation. The viva-voce on dissertation paper is conducted by a board of examiners consisting of the respective guide and an external expert. Any topic relating to the current problem of L&IS for dissertation can be selected by the students in consultation with the teacher concerned. The students are allowed sixty days time for the submission of the dissertation after the completion of final theory and practical examinations. To pass the examination a candidate must obtain a minimum of 40 per cent including internal assessment marks in each theory paper and 45 per cent marks plus internal assessment marks in each practical paper.

6.3 *Jadavpur University*

Paper	Title of the paper	Exam. marks	Internal assessment
I.	Universe of Subjects & Research Methodology	75	25
II.	Information Science and Information Sources	75	25
III.	Group A: Depth classn (theory)	40	10
	Group B: Advanced cataloguing (theory)	40	10
IV.	Group A: Depth classification (Practice)	40	10
	Group B: Advanced cataloging (Practice)	40	10
V.	Information Storage and Retrieval	75	25
VI.	Management of Library and Information Centres & Systems	75	25
VII.	Elective paper: (one of the following) (a) Computer application in library (b) Public library system (c) Academic library system (d) Research & Technical library system		
VIII.	Project report (including 20 marks for viva-voce)	80	

The scheme of the course content has been detailed into 8 papers, consisting of 100 marks in each paper. Papers III and IV have been divided into two groups consisting of theoretical and practical. Paper VIII entitled 'Project Report' on any aspect of L&IS assigned by the teacher concerned. Twentyfive marks are set apart in paper I, II, V, VI and VII, whereas 20 marks are allotted for paper III and IV as internal assessment. Again in paper VII, 20 marks are kept reserved for viva-voce on the project report, and 80 marks for entire project prepared and submitted by the students. The viva-voce on 'Project Report' is conducted by a board of examiners comprising the respective teacher of the department and an external. The project will have to be submitted by the students positively within sixty days after the last date of final examination every year. The qualifying marks for passing the examination are at least 40 per cent marks in each paper. Minimum marks to secure a place in the first class is 60 per cent and the second division 40 per cent of the total marks.

6.4 *Vidyasagar University*

Paper	Title of the paper	Exam. marks	Duration of exam.
I.	Organisation of Knowledge Group A: Classification (Theory) Group B: Cataloguing (Theory)	100	4 hrs
II.	Library planning and management	100	4 hrs
III.	Bibliographic organisation and control.	100	4 hrs
IV.	Library automation, Information storage and Retrieval	100	4 hrs
V.	Group (1): Literature of Humanities and Social Scs.	50	
	Group (2): Literature of Science and Technology	50	4 hrs
VI.	Part 1: Classification (Practice)	50	3 hrs
	Part 2: Cataloguing (Practice)	50	3 hrs
VII.	Literature Survey	100	
VIII.	Dissertation	80	
	Viva Voce	20	

The syllabus structure reveals that the courses of study have been divided into eight papers, and papers I to IV carry 100 marks and shall be of four hours duration. Papers V and VI have been split up into two parts, each paper consisting of 50 marks. The examination of each part in paper VI holds separately and shall be of duration of three hours. No formal classes are held in paper VII and VIII. In paper VII a literature survey is to be made by the students on current topic related to any subject recommended by the teacher. Similarly, in paper VIII, a dissertation is to be prepared by the student on any aspect relating to the current problems of L&IS assigned by the concerned teacher. No internal assessment marks have been prescribed in the scheme of papers. Only 20 marks are set apart for viva-voce on the dissertation. The viva-voce on dissertation is conducted by a board of examiners including the internal teacher and an external. The pass requirement is a minimum of 30 per cent in each theoretical and practical paper and in aggregate 40 per cent of the total marks.

7. **Observations**

With the development of new library techniques and rapid changes in L&IS education, careful attention needs to be given in designing and structuring of the syllabi of the library schools. After close analysis of the curricula of these schools, it is observed that no uniform pattern is maintained in regard to course-content of the Master degree level. Different patterns of syllabus have been followed by the different universities. Papers I, II, III, IV, and VI have been stuck to the traditional course contents in Calcutta, though it has introduced two years course, and in paper V the expanding dimensions of the discipline such as informatics, information communication, computer application in libraries, use of micrographics have not been incorporated in the course of study. Besides there is a considerable variation in the number of compulsory and optional papers.

All library schools except Calcutta agree that 'classification' and 'cataloguing' should be half paper both in theory and practice. Calcutta University recommended these two papers as a full paper in theory and half paper in practice. All curricula in both the papers are more or less comprehensive. Burdwan, Jadavpur, and Vidyasagar provide for a comparative study of both CC and UDC in classification (practical). Calcutta has a provision for detailed study of UDC only in practical paper. In Cataloguing theory the syllabi drafted by all the universities are almost identical and prescribed detailed study of the theoretical aspects of the paper. In practical paper all schools excluding Calcutta have made a provision for the comparative study of both AACR II and CCC. But Calcutta makes the study of only AACR II. However, the practices followed in regard to the evaluation for both practicals vary widely from school to school.

The conventional paper Universe of Knowledge/Subjects and Research Methodology which has been introduced as a compulsory course by Burdwan and Jadavpur does not find place in the course design of Calcutta and Vidyasagar Universities. Similarly there is no paper of Information Science and Information Sources in both Calcutta and Vidyasagar Universities. Burdwan and Jadavpur both study this paper as a full paper. All the universities introduced a paper on Information Storage and Retrieval. Calcutta and Vidyasagar have a provision for a paper as Literature of Humanities or Social Sciences, and Literature of Science and Technology, to be studied as a combined paper. Burdwan and Jadavpur make no provision for this paper. Vidyasagar makes a provision for a paper entitled Bibliographic Organisation and Control. But it omits many important aspects such as UBC, UAP, the role played by international organisations in bibliographic control from the syllabus. Burdwan, Calcutta and Jadavpur prescribe elective subjects consisting of four/five groups from which any one of the groups is to be taken by the students. Jadavpur also introduced a paper on Computer Application in Libraries as an elective paper. But there is no provision for elective subjects in Vidyasagar. In addition, it introduced a paper on Literature Survey. Calcutta does not have a full paper on Dissertation/Project work.

It is evident from the above analysis that Calcutta and Vidyasagar do not follow a unified pattern in designing the courses of study and structuring the papers, nor do they follow the model syllabus recommended by the UGC Review Committee. Even there is glaring disparity between the provision of topics and contents prescribed in different papers by these universities. The nomenclature of most of the papers also differs from that of Burdwan and Jadavpur. Calcutta is the first to take lead in introducing two years M Lib Sc course at par with the Master's degree course in other subjects in the campus. But the uniformity and consistency have not been maintained in the structure of papers and even in the distribution of marks. While Master's degree courses in other disciplines recommend 800 total marks, the university prescribes 1000 total marks in M Lib Sc. However, it seems that the curriculum has been drafted in the light of the American schools, and Vidyasagar appears to be mostly influenced by the Calcutta school.

On the other hand Burdwan and Jadavpur provide a most comprehensive course-module in all aspects of L&IS education in general. The nomenclature and contents of the papers (both core and elective subjects) in these two universities are almost the same and they follow the all India pattern in designing and structuring the courses of study. From an overall analysis it transpires that Burdwan and Jadavpur courses follow the most useful syllabus on the pattern of the UGC Review Committee (1965) and UGC model syllabus (1982).

Further the present study reveals that there is no uniformity in regard to course content, method of evaluation, distribution of marks, admission criteria to the master degree level, duration of the course etc.

in these universities. Lack of a uniform set of norms and standards prevails in the teaching techniques of various core and elective subjects, in the distribution of minimum marks in passing the examination, and even in the internal assessments and other project works.

8 Suggestions

A close study of the different curricula module and structure of papers in Master's degree level in West Bengal universities has been made in this paper, and to improve the quality of standard of L&IS education in the country, the following suggestions have been detailed here:

(1) A proper balance and standard must be maintained in designing the curricula in MLIS level, duration of course, method of teaching, examination, physical facilities, admission criteria, intake and teacher-student ratio etc.
(2) The syllabi of Calcutta and Vidyasagar Universities should be restructured in conformity with the recommendations of the UGC Review Committee and UGC Panel (1982). The contents and nomenclature of some of the papers of these schools should be updated and changed to reflect the new thoughts, ideas and growing needs of L&IS education. In short a thorough change in the curricula incorporating new technologies and trends is essential.
(3) The coordination and cooperation among the library schools should be strengthened by exchanging specialists, experienced teachers and faculty members.
(4) Regular seminars, refresher/orientation courses, summer institutes and workshops should be conducted regularly for updating the knowledge of the faculty members in the context of rapid advancement in the field of L&IS.
(5) Provision for adequate fund for research should be made available to the universities by providing research fellowships as in other disciplines.
(6) A national centre for research in L&IS should be established in order to improve the quality of research in L&IS and which will also support and guide research programmes.
(7) Manpower survey may be conducted periodically to identify the number, nature and level of personnel required so that training programmes at higher level may be recast according to the re-

quirements of the libraries.

(8) The teacher-student ratio recommended by the UGC Review Committee should be maintained to achieve effective and efficient teaching.

(9) Finally one accreditation agency should be set up at the national level which will lay down standards for admission, duration of the course, curriculum design, teacher-student ratio, library facilities, teaching techniques, evaluation method and physical quarters etc. Such standard will help to obtain the qualitative and quantitative aspects of the course.

13

NEED OF TWO YEARS INTEGRATED MLIS COURSE IN GUJARAT

K.H. SHUKLA

1. Introduction

On the 5th January 1887, the first library school in the world, the School of Library Economy came into existence at Columbia College in New York city of the USA. Just after twenty-four years, Gujarat was fortunate enough to have a training course in librarianship in 1911 in Baroda, under the guidance of W.A. Borden, which was also the first school in the country. Thus, the need of professionally qualified personnel to manage and to run libraries efficiently and effectively was recognised for the first time in Gujarat, way back in 1911.

The first university level Library Science education was started in 1937 at the Madras University by S.R. Ranganathan. The MS University of Baroda started the course in Gujarat in 1957. In all out of ten universities of the state, seven universities are offering BLIS programme, and five universities are offering MLIS programme.

2 BLIS and MLIS Programme in Gujarat

The following table provides the complete information of BLIS and MLIS programmes started in various universities of Gujarat.

University	Year of establishment	Year of starting BLIS	Year of starting MLIS
MS University, Baroda	1949	1957	1986
Gujarat Univ., Ahmedabad	1950	1964	1986
SP Univ., Vallabh Vidyanagar	1955	1982	1988

Gujarat Vidyapeeth, Ahmedabad	1963*	1988	1986
Saurashtra Univ., Rajkot	1967	1975	1987
South Gujarat Univ., Surat	1967	1986	—
Bhavanagar Univ., Bhavanagar	1978	1980	—

* Gujarat Vidyapeeth was established in 1920 by Mahatma Gandhi, and was recognised as deemed to be university in 1963.

It reveals that during 1950s, 1960s and 1970s one school per decade came into existence whereas during 1980s only four new schools came into existence with L&IS programme. Here it is also surprising that the Gujarat Vidyapeeth has started first MLIS course in 1986, and thereafter BLIS in 1988.

3. MLIS Syllabus

Let us examine the pattern of syllabi of these five universities.

In the MS University, Baroda, MLIS syllabus is divided in three groups. Group-A consists of four papers, each of 100 marks. Group-B consists of dissertation of 300 marks or four term papers each of 75 marks. Group-C consists of viva-voce of 100 marks.

Gujarat Vidyapeeth, Ahmedabad, has a different pattern. It is a two-year time study course with classes on every Sunday from 10 am to 4 pm, with one year semester system. In the first semester i.e. in the first year are held four papers each of 100 marks, and the second semester i.e. second year, three papers each of 100 marks plus a dissertation and viva-voce of 200 marks.

SP University, Vallabh Vidyanagar has a two-year part-time course consisting of four semesters each of six months. Classes are held on every Sunday from 10 am to 4.30 pm. During the first three semesters two papers each of 100 marks are taught per semester. Fourth semester consists of one paper of 100 marks plus dissertation and viva-voce of 100 marks.

Gujarat University and Saurashtra University have similar syllabi having seven papers, in which five papers of theory, and two of practicals, each of 100 marks, and a dissertation of 100 marks, making the total 800 marks, to work within an academic year.

It seems very obvious from these different courses that MS University, Baroda has based its syllabus on Bombay-Pune pattern, while Gujarat University, Saurashtra University, and SP University have based their syllabi on the normal pattern, which is prevalent in the universities of Delhi, Dharwar, Kolhapur etc.

The MLIS syllabus of Gujarat Vidyapeeth is unique in the sense that too much weightage has been given to various aspects of information which overlap in three papers, while practical aspects of advanced classification and cataloguing are conspicuous by their absence.

4. Two-year Integrated MLIS Course

Advancement in the fields of human learning and knowledge and also in the fields of information recording and retrieval through media technology, and increasing demand for MLIS degree holders necessitates a thorough rethinking and restructuring of L&IS education in Gujarat.

The two-year integrated MLIS programme can be considered in four semesters, each semester being of about sixteen weeks and four periods a day. First three semesters comprise four papers each of 100 marks. The fourth semesters can have three papers of 100 marks each and dissertation of 100 marks. Thus the total marks would be 1600. Those who are successful in the first two semesters and do not want to continue their study further could be awarded BLIS degree. Similarly practising librarians who are already BLIS and interested to improve their qualifications will be eligible to get admission in the second year i.e. third and fourth semester.

4.1 *Two Year Integrated MLIS Syllabus*

The semesterwise two-year integrated MLIS syllabus break-up of the papers would be as under:

First Semester

1. Library and society
2. Reference and information sources
3. Reference and information services
4. Information systems and programme

Second Semester

1. Library classification theory
2. Library classification practice
3. Library cataloguing theory

4. Library cataloguing practice

Third Semester

1. Universe of knowledge: Its development and structure
2. Research methodology and system analysis
3. Information storage and retrieval
4. Library planning and management techniques

Fourth Semester

1. Computer applications in libraries
2. Information technology
3. Library system: (elective) any one of the following: (a) Public; (b) Academic; (c) Research and special; (d) Law; (e) Medical; and (f) Agricultural

4.2. *Outlines of Curriculum*

The papers described in semester one and two need not require any elaboration as they are of routine pattern. The outlines of each paper of third and fourth semester are as under:

4.2.1 *Third Semester*

Paper 1: Universe of Knowledge: Its Development and Structure.

It is essential to acquaint the students of L&IS with the growth and development of knowledge and subjects, research methods, organization of research etc. Following topics may be provided in the paper: (a) Growth and development of knowledge; (b) Growth and development of scholarship; (c) Development of research: Fundamental and applied; (d) Methods of pure sciences, applied science, social sciences, and humanities; (e) Organisation of research in different countries including India, UK, USA and USSR.

Paper 2: Research Methodology and System Analysis

(a) Various methods of research; (b) Research methodology and various disciplines of universe of knowledge; (c) Problems of research and techniques; (d) Basic concept of system analysis; (e) Role of system analysis; (f) System analysis, evaluation and implementation of system design.

Paper 3: Information Storage and Retrieval

(a) Basic concept of information storage and retrieval; (b) General theory of indexing; (c) Content analysis, abstracting, digesting and other condensation methods; (d) Subject indexing including history and development; (e) Indexing languages: Thesaurus, thesauro facet etc; (f) Methodology to develop a thesaurus; (g) Pre-coordinate and post-coordinate system and indexing: PRECIS, POPSI etc; (h) Special types of indexing; KWIC, KWOC, Cyclic Etc.

Paper 4: Library Planning and Management Techniques

To acquaint the students with the library planning and its management techniques, the topics may be covered as: (a) Principles of planning and management, its application to library; (b) Methods of application; (c) Planning, designing and development of library; (d) Operation, control and evaluation of library services etc.

4.2.2 *Fourth Semester*

Paper 1: Computer Application in Libraries

Keeping in view the impact of computer technology in our day to day life it is essential to acquaint students with the computer application in libraries and information centres which may include: (a) Data selection, file organisation, data structure, database management; (b) Programming languages: their characteristics and use; (c) Automatic text processing; (d) Computer hardware and software development; (e) Study of computer use in the context of libraries, information centres etc.

Note: It also requires consultation with computer scientist in incorporating details of each topic.

Paper 2: Information Technology

To provide the students with a basic knowledge of the application of: (a) Computer technology and communication techniques; (b) Reprography and printing technology to information system and services; (c) Information theory, coding etc; (d) Planning and design of information technology application to libraries and information centres.

Paper 3: Library System (elective)

Topics based on the types of library systems:

Paper 4: Dissertation

The aim should be to develop ability of the student to identify problem areas, apply methods of research and design experiments in finding solutions to problems; to formulate research proposals; and to effectively present a dissertation on an assigned topic.

4.3 *Admission Policy and Criteria for MLIS Course*

Admission criteria for two-year integrated MLIS course should be of such type which may minimise wastage in professional education. Keeping in view all aspects related to L&IS education in Gujarat, 10 to 15 students may be admitted in the first semester to produce qualitative manpower for the profession. While selecting students for MLIS course it is essential that it should be on the basis of merit as well as their performance in the aptitude test.

5. **L&IS Faculty in Gujarat**

Out of seven universities of the State, only two universities have full-time L&IS faculty members. The MS University has one Reader and one lecturer. Gujarat University has two lecturers whereas in the remaining universities the librarian of the university as a part time coordinator is assigned the teaching responsibility over and above his administrative duties. Very often it is felt that the librarian of the university is a busy administrator and he has enough work of his library. In this situation he is unable to give justice to teaching assignments. Hence it is essential to have at least four to five full-time L&IS faculty members, of which at least one should be Professor, one Reader, and two to three lecturers. On an average each teacher will have 12 periods of work load per week.

6. **Conclusion**

From the above discussion it is crystal clear that the future of BLIS holders in Gujarat is dark. The MLIS programme, started in 1986, has ample opportunity in the State. Hence it is essential to develop and produce qualitative manpower in the State. MLIS programme should be of two-year integrated course to meet the needs of the profession in Gujarat. It is also essential to strengthen the teaching programme admitting more full-time teaches in the department of various universities. In view of the inflation in the availability of library personnel in Gujarat no other university should be permitted to start L&IS programme so as to avoid further worsening of the situation.

14

PROJECT ON METHODOLOGY OF STUDY OF SUBJECTS: An Experience

(Miss) K. NAVALANI

Dr S.R. Ranganathan was the architect of curricula of Library Science education in India. "Education and Training in Library and Information Science owe to him (Dr Ranganathan) and for that matter library profession in India is his making to a very large extent"[1], rightly remarked late Rajagopalan. During his tenure in the University of Delhi from 1947-55, Master in Library Science was started.[2] He was also responsible for introducing the paper: "Universe of Knowledge: Structure and Development" in its curriculum in 1948.[3] The UGC Committee on Library Science Education with Ranganathan as chairman recommended a model syllabus for M Lib Sc which included this paper.[4] A survey conducted by Prof. P.N. Kaula, indicated that the paper" is being taught in 24 universities, and in modified version and under changed nomenclature in another four universities. Bombay University was the only exception to this.[5] Thus, the paper is being taught for the last forty years in India universities at Master's level.

To take stock of the situation, a UGC sponsored national seminar of four days was exclusively devoted to the paper and its relevance in the curriculum of MLISc course.[6] Hardly, any paper in Library and Information Science has gained such an importance.

As we all know, Dr Ranganathan founded the DRTC, Bangalore, and he was associated with it till he breathed his last. Dr Ranganathan's associate in the DRTC, Prof G. Bhattacharya, proposed in the seminar that in the changed situation, 'Project on Study of Subjects' be included in courses in library and information science. According to him, " an information scientist is required to provide information work and service predominantly pertaining to a subject or a group of subjects, which calls for necessary and sufficient knowledge of the special facets of the subject or of the group of subjects concerned".[7] Academic background of a professional may provide knowledge for a subject(s) in which one has to provide information. Further, a professional has to help in search for research, which takes one to new fields, in which one can hardly get academic background education. "The whole situation is peculiar", pleads Prof. Bhattacharya, "That it warrants the information scientist to be always capable of acquiring knowledge of the special facets of any subject, as fast as practicable, whenever the need arises, and of keeping it uptodate throughout his professional life with the subject or a group of subjects concerned".[8] But, in his opinion, such an approach towards a subject would be of 'subject generalisation' and not of 'subject specialisation'. And the methodology of gaining knowledge about the subject, as Prof Bhattacharya proposes, is through self study, by preparing a subject. He has also suggested contents of the project and provided proforma for the collection and organisation of information about the subject".[9]

In the National Seminar on Universe of Knowledge held in 1986, in Hyderabad, it was resolved to introduce 'Project on Study of Subjects' as an alternative to paper 'Universe of Knowledge/Subjects' in some universities. Punjabi University was in the process of framing its syllabus for MLISc. It took up the challenge and was perhaps the first school to include the paper at Master's level in any university in India. Therefore, it will be pertinent to share our experience with the teachers in this seminar.

Till now, two sessions have been completed and the third session is half its way. In the first and second sessions (1987-88 and 1988-89), the following topics were covered:

(1) Psychoanalysis
(2) Genetics
(3) Information Technology
(4) Operations Research
(5) Mass Communication
(6) Marketing
(7) Culture
(8) Industrial Chemistry
(9) Biotechnology
(10) Organization

(11) Public relations
(12) Structuralism
(13) Astrophysics

We have semester system and the paper is the first in the first semester. As the paper is to be cleared in the first semester, the rule regarding submission of the project is: Every candidate has to submit it fifteen days before the commencement of the examination of the first semester.

It is essential for any work to be evaluated for making improvements/changes, if required. Therefore, to get feedback from the students, who completed their projects in the last two sessions, a questionnaire was administered to them. Only 50 per cent of these students, who are working in the Punjabi University, and were readily available, were approached for the purpose. A few questions were asked, to seek their opinions about the project and problems faced by them in completing it.

To the question: Do you find the project work interesting/taxing/boring/so so, only one of the respondents replied – Interesting. Two of them found it boring: another two – so so; and one taxing.

The second question was: Problems faced by you in preparing the project. They were all unanimously of the opinion that time for the project was very short. Second problem, according to five of them, was of non-availability of materials for compiling such a project. In other words, a good library collection is *sine qua-non* for such a project work. Three of them felt that understanding and comprehension of the new subject not only took time but was a difficult job. Two of them complained about the non-availability of guidance, and one had a problem, because of inter-disciplinary nature of the subject.

Next question was: Which of the chapters of the ject posed more problems. Two of the respondents replied: Research trends and development; two – terminological development; and one – Human resources.

However, their opinions were divided on the usefulness of the project. Three of them perceived it to be not of any use to them in the university library where they were working; while three found it useful; and one replied – to some extent.

Besides, opinions of some of the members of the faculty were also elicited, informally in this regard.

There cannot be two opinions, that a student has to devote more time and expend greater effort on the project work as compared to a paper. As MLISc started late in the first session, 1987-88, so the period of submitting the project was extended by one month, after the commencement of the examination. Only one student submitted the project within this period. Rest of the candidates submitted their projects almost two months after the time limit. In the second session, 1988-89 students could submit their projects more than three months after its due date of submission. The state of affairs is no better this session also. The time taken by students for completion of their projects during the second semester affects other programmes, papers and the dissertation work which they have to submit in the second semester.

Secondly, the sources are very limited at Patiala. And the students are at a disadvantage to tap the adjoining libraries because of very tight time schedule of semester system. Keeping these facts in mind, the topic 'Special classification' proposed by Prof Bhattacharya in his paper of 1975[10] had to be dropped from the second session of the course.

Thirdly, though the students admitted to the course score high marks, yet over all level of intelligence and understanding of some of them is not up to the mark. Particularly, students who have humanities background, face more difficulties, as is our impression. As the subject of the project is totally new for them, so some of them find it difficult to comprehend and at the initial stage feel lost.

The project work is of use to those who join special libraries or are/will be actively involved in search for research. Perhaps, those of the professionals, engaged in acquisition etc work, do not find it useful. It may be mentioned here, that 40 per cent of the respondents did not consider the paper 'Universe of Knowledge' useful to their work; as reported by Sood and Jotwani.[11]

In view of the above facts, in my humble opinion, inclusion of paper – Project of Study of Subjects – at MLISc level, within the very tight framework of the semester system needs second look.

REFERENCES

1. Rajagopalan, T.S., (Ed.) Ranganathan's Philosophy: Assessment, Impact and Relevance. *Proceedings of the International Conference*. New Delhi, Vikas, 1986 p. viii.
2. Krishan Kumar, An outline of Universe of Knowledge course: A few suggestions. In Raju, A.A.N. and Laxman Rao, N. (Ed.) National Seminar on Universe of Knowledge, its relevance in the curriculum of MLISc course, 25-28 November,

1986. Seminar papers. Hyderabad. Department of Library and Information Science, Osmania University, 1986. Cyclostyled, p. co - 1.

3. Kaula, P.N., Study of universe of knowledge: Analysis, trends and developments. In Raju, A.A.N. and Laxman Rao, N. (Ed.) *Ibid.* p. Cf 1.
4. UGC, Review Committee, Library Science in Indian universities, 1965.
5. Kaula, P.N., *Op cit.*
6. National seminar on Universe of Knowledge, its structure and development: its relevance in the curriculum of MLISc course, 25-28 November, 1986. Organised by the Department of Library and Information Science, Osmania University, Hyderabad.
7. Bhattacharya, G., 'Project on Study of Subjects'. *Library Science with Slant to Documentation*, V. 12, No 3, 1975 Sept. p 66.
8. *Ibid.* p 66.
9. *Ibid.*
10. *Ibid.*
11. Sood, S.P. and Jotwani, D., Universe of Knowledge: Should it be included in the curriculum of MLISc course: A survey. In Raju, A.A.N. and Laxman Rao, N., (ed.) *op cit.*

15

A CRITICAL APPRAISAL OF THE MLIS CURRICULA OF THE UNIVERSITIES OF PUNJAB AND CHANDIGARH

JAGTAR SINGH

1. The Problem

The topic of Library and Information Science education has been selected with a view to have a close look at the Master of Library and Information Science (MLIS) curricula of the Universities of Punjab and Chandigarh. The author is of the view that since the MLIS course leads to a post-graduate degree, it must have a curriculum which prepares the professionals to adapt to the change and challenges of the new information society.

1.1 *Limitations*

The study is confined to the Punjab University, Chandigarh; Punjabi University, Patiala; and Gurunanak Dev University, Amritsar only. Further, it specifically speaks about MLIS curricula with a few cross references to BLIS curricula at certain points. A systems approach is a pre-requisite to have a comprehensive view of the library and information science education and its amelioration. Hence, along with the critical appraisal of MLIS curricula of these universities, the other relevant facets of the problem have also been touched upon.

2. Methodology

For data collection the latest prospectus-cum-syallabus of each university were discussed with the colleagues to know their views. The MLIS students of Punjabi University were also interviewed. Besides, relevant professional literature was studied to crystallize the views on this problem.

2.1 *Data Analysis*

Punjab University, Chandigarh; Punjabi University, Patiala; and Guru Nanak Dev University, Amritsar were established during the years 1948, 1962, and 1969 respectively. The MLIS courses were introduced in these universities during the academic years 1970-71, 1987-88 and 1984-85 respectively. It is obvious that Punjabi University was established before the GND University, Amritsar, but the MLIS course was introduced during the academic year 1987-88.

3. **Objectives of the Course**

The objectives of the course in these universities have been stated as under:

Punjab University, Chandigarh:[1] To acquaint the students with:

(1) The evolution and pattern of universe of knowledge and research methodology;
(2) Documentation work; and
(3) The advanced techniques of modern librarianship and research problems.

Punjabi University, Patiala:[2] To produce mangers and thinkers for:

(1) Planning and decision-making for large libraries, and information systems and services; and
(2) To expose students to research and its methodology, in the field of L&IS

Gurunanak Dev University, Amritsar:[3] To acquaint the students with:

(1) The evolution and pattern of universe of knowledge and research methodology;
(2) The documentation and information retrieval techniques and systems; and

(3) The advanced techniques of modern librarianship (including application of computers), and management and administration of select types of libraries.

Even at a cursory look, one can find that the GND University has determined the objectives similar to those of Punjab University, Chandigarh with minor modifications. The objectives of Punjabi University, Patiala seem more uptodate.

3.1 *Scheme of Papers (see Annexure)*

An analysis of the scheme of papers throws light on the fact that the curricula of the Punjab University and GND University are tradition-oriented and that of the Punjabi University is innovation-oriented. But both are not free from their flaws. While the components of universe of knowledge, depth classification, and advanced cataloguing in Punjab and GND Universities seem partially irrelevant, the paper Information Storage and Retrieval at Punjabi University needs details. The paper Computer application in libraries and information centres in all the three universities needs rethinking.

As regards the element of options, Punjab University provides maximum number of options, i.e. 13, followed by Punjabi University with 8, and the GND University with 7 options. The first paper of Punjabi University, viz., Methodology of Studying Subjects its a new feature. But it has its own problems. In semester system, it is very difficult for the students to finish both the projects (first semester) and dissertation (second semester) in time. Hence the students of the three batches have sought extensions to submit their projects/dissertations. Time lag, non-availability of adequate resources and comparatively dull intake are a few problems related to this paper (Methodology of Studying Subjects). Besides the traditional options in all the three universities, Punjab University has two more options, i.e., Operations Research and Systems Analysis, and Education for Library and Information Science. Punjab University provides more choice to the students in the sixth paper 'Bibliography and Literature'. These additional options are Bibliography and Literature in Medical Sciences or in Agricultural Sciences or in Engineering and Technology. But the main point for consideration is not the options on record. But the options the students are allowed. It is a hard fact that the size of the faculty and their specializations are the main impediments in making this system of options work. One more factor is the non-availability of adequate resources to teach these options effectively.

Since it was specified in the very beginning that restructuring the curriculum alone will not solve all the problems it would be better to discuss the related aspects of L&IS education. These are highlighted in the following paragraphs.

4. Admission Criteria

The students who join the MLIS course form an important component of the system. In all the three universities, the criterion for admission is as under. In Punjab University it is post-graduate diploma in Library Science (one year course) or Punjab University BLIS or any equivalent degree or diploma of any other university with 50 per cent marks. In Punjabi University it is BLIS with 50 per cent or such examination from any other university with 50 per cent marks and M.A./M.Sc with at least 50 per cent marks or such examination passed from any other university with at least 50 per cent marks. At GND University it is a B Lib Sc with M.A./M.Com both 50 per cent from the same university or from any other university. Besides, the students are to pass an admission test and fulfil other conditions laid down by the Board of Control.

The positive feature of GND University is the admission test, but its drawback is that it is held only for Library Classification (Theory) and Library Cataloguing (Theory). Among all the three universities, Punjab University does not insist on post-graduate degree for admission to MLIS.

4.1 *Duration*

All the three universities follow semester system with two semesters in an academic year.

4.2 *Intake*

The total number of seats in MLIS is 16,6, and 10 respectively in Punjab University, Punjabi University, and GND University.

4.3 *Faculty*

The sanctioned strength at Punjab University is one Reader, and five lecturers; at Punjabi University one Reader, and four lecturers; and at GND University it is again one Reader, and four lecturers. But the present position of the faculty in these universities by virtue of merit promotion is as under. Two readers, and four lecturers including one re-employed reader at Punjab University; one Professor, one Reader, and three lecturers (one post is lying vacant) and (one re-employed lecturer at Punjabi University); and three Readers and two lecturers at GND University. The painful fact is that the sanctioned strength of all the universities does not provide for the post of Professor.

4.4 *Accommodation and Equipment*

The department of L&IS at Punjab University is housed in a newly constructed building and has suitable accommodation. Both Punjabi and GND Universities are not having adequate accommodation. Punjab University has one overhead projector; and the Punjabi University has two overhead projectors and a PC/XT is going to be installed very shortly. The problem is to house it in a suitable place with suitable environment. GND University does not have any projector.

5. **Suggestions**

To adopt to the change and challenge of information society, the objectives of the MLIS course should be redefined. There should be a shift from process-centred curricula to community's need-centred curricula. Our curricula should be in a position to produce professionals who are able to understand and satisfy the information needs of particular communities of users. Benefits must be accrued from the incremental, conceptional, and skill-oriented models of curriculum development.

The curriculum should be restructured in the context of changes which are taking place in the information society. The papers such as Universe of Knowledge, Library Classification, Library Cataloguing, Methodology of Studying Subjects' etc. should be reviewed. For the paper 'Methodology of Studying Subjects' either the time limit should be increased or the paper should be made optional. The number of optional papers should be increased to produce specialists in the profession. The faculty with special academic background should be recruited and trained to teach these papers effectively.

The training/practice aspect of the L&IS course should be given more importance. For brilliant intake, an admission test must be held for MLIS course, just like in other professional courses in the university. At least one micro computer should be given to each L&IS department, and a few faculty members must be trained be handle it. In view of the above observations, it is suggested that standards must be worked out, and a national committee may be constituted to develop a model L&IS curriculum. A systems approach must be adopted to provide a quality L&IS education to the concerned members of the society.

REFERENCES

1. Punjab University, Chandigarh, Department of Library and Information Science. *Prospectus cum admission form for BLIS and MLIS course*, 1989-90, 39p.
2. Punjabi University, Patiala, Publication Bureau. *Ordinances and outlines of tests, syllabi and courses of reading for MLIS (semester system)*, 1989-90 and 1990-91 sessions. 29 p.
3. Gurunanakdev University, Amritsar, Department of L&IS. *Prospectus cum syllabus*, 1989-90, 34 p.

ANNEXURE

Master of Library and Information Science (MLIS): Scheme of Papers

Punjab University, Chandigarh

1. Universe of knowledge and research methodology.
2. Information storage and retrieval.
3. Information systems and programmes.
   (a) Library organisation and administration (Public libraries)
   OR
   (b) Library organisation and administration (Academic libraries)
   OR
   (c) Library organisation and administration (Special libraries)

4. Advanced classification (practice)
5. Advanced cataloguing (practice)
6. (a) Bibliography and literature in humanities
   OR
   (b) Bibliography and literature in social sciences
   OR
   (c) Bibliography and literature in natural sciences
   OR
   (d) Bibliography and literature in medical sciences
   OR
   (e) Bibliography and literature in engineering and technology
   OR
   (f) Bibliography and literature in agricultural sciences
7. Depth classification (Theory)
8. Dissertation
   OR
   Computer application in libraries/information centres
   OR
   Operations research and systems analysis
   OR
   Education for Library and Information Science

Gurunanakdev University, Amritsar

1. Universe of subjects and research methodology
2. (a) Depth classification (theory)
   (b) Depth classification (practice)
3. Information storage and retrieval
4. Bibliography and literature survey
5. (a) Advanced cataloguing (theory)
   (b) Advanced cataloguing (practice)
6. Library organisation and management
7. Computer application in libraries
8. Dissertation

Punjabi University, Patiala

1. Methodology of studying subjects
2. Research methods.
3. Scientific management of libraries
4. (i) Information and literature survey in sciences

   OR

   (ii) Information and literature survey in Humanities

   OR

   (iii) Information and literature survey in social sciences
5. Information storage and retrieval
6. (i) Library and information system (Public)
   (ii) Library and information system (Academic)
   (iii) Library and information system (Special)
7. Computer application in library and information systems

   OR

   Information systems and services
8. Dissertation

16

NEED OF SPECIALIZATION AT MLIS LEVEL

K.J. MAJUMDAR and K.H. SHUKLA

1. Introduction

Need of L&IS education was recognised as early as in later 19th century at the global level, and in India it was recognised in 1911. Dr. S. R. Ranganathan was considered as an architect of L&IS syllabus in the country. The present curriculum of L&IS is unable to meet the challenges made upon the profession. As Master of Library and Information Science (MLIS) education is meant for senior professionals, it needs specialisation in various aspects of library profession. L&IS education is now on the take off stage requiring thorough restructuring.

2. Scope

Scope of the present paper aims to suggest need of specialisation at MLIS level, with a view to keeping pace with increasing specialisation in every field of knowledge and meeting challenges and providing leadership to the profession in general and the library in particular.

Further, the existing L&IS education pattern in India and the feasibility and scope of the need of specialisation at MLIS syllabus has been elaborated.

3. Need for Specialisation at MLIS Level

In every walk of life now-a-days there is a burning desire for achieving specialisation. In every field of human knowledge, in very many professions too there is a rat race for specialisation. In professional education also specialisation seems to be the most necessity to meet challenges. The need for specialisation in L&IS education is also felt now a days because of increasing complexity in the library services and demands of users of the library.

The present concept of library science has been revolutionalized by the need of library services and the challenges made upon by the clientele. During the past century substantial literature in various aspects of L&IS and library services has come out. Simultaneously increasing specialisation in various fields of knowledge demands specialised service from their libraries and it has necessitated the need for specialisation in L&IS education.

4. Existing MLIS Education in India

The present L&IS education in Indian Universities is of two-tier type, each of one-year i.e. BLIS and MLIS. The chief constraints of these two-tier L&IS courses is over-lapping and more weightage is on theory orientation rather than practice orientation. The present MLIS syllabus offers seven to eight papers, each of hundred marks, and dissertation or project report ranges between 100 to 300 marks including viva-voce. 400 to 500 marks are devoted to the papers like classification theory and practice, cataloguing theory and practice, and universe of knowledge whereas 200 to 300 marks are devoted to library systems and information science. It is also observed that information science is being taught in the absence of information technology, which is meaningless. It reveals that the present syllabi of MLIS aims to produce more theoreticians and teachers of L&IS rather than the practicing librarians to meet the challenges against the library profession.

5. Proposed Syllabi for MLIS

MLIS education aims to produce senior professionals who have to face library practice oriented problems rather than theory oriented problems and they vary from library to library. The present MLIS syllabi fails to resolve the problems of the present library service as it is much theory oriented.

The present MLIS syllabus offers one elective paper on any one library systems which fails to give justice to the particular library system. Various library techniques, systems and operations cannot be covered in only one paper of hundred marks. It is essential to provide opportunity to make study of various specialised areas of L&IS. MLIS syllabi must provide thorough knowledge in specific specialised area.

The MLIS syllabi should be divided into three groups. Group one offers four compulsory papers. Group two offers three effective papers subject to specialized areas of L&IS, and group three consists of dissertation and viva-voce.

5.1 *Compulsory Papers (Group one)*

In MLIS, Group one consists of four compulsory papers which aim to planning library and produce library personnel to meet the problems of library services in general perspective, and to meet the present requirements of the clientele. They are:

(1) Library planning and management techniques.
(2) Research methodology and systems analysis.
(3) Information storage and retrieval.
(4) Information technology.

5.1.1 *Outlines of Compulsory Papers*

The papers under group one are compulsory papers the outline of each is as under:

Paper 1. Library Planning and Management Techniques

To acquaint the students with the library planning and its management techniques the following topics may be covered: (a) Principles of planning and management, its application to library; (b) Methods of application; (c) Planning, designing and development of library; (d) Operation control and evaluation of library services etc.

Paper 2. Research Methodology and Systems Analysis

To acquaint students with the research methodology and systems analysis, the following topics may be covered. (a) Various methods of research; (b) Research methodology and various disciplines of universe of knowledge; (c) Problems of research and techniques; (d) Basic concepts of systems' analysis; (e) role of systems analysis; (f) systems analysis evaluation and implementation of system design.

Paper 3. Information Storage and Retrieval

To acquaint students with information service; storage and retrieval techniques, the following topics may be covered:

(a) Basic concepts of information storage and retrieval; (b) General theory of indexing; (c) Content analysis; abstracting, digesting and other condensation methods; (d) subject indexing including history and development; (e) Indexing languages: thesaurus, thesauro facet etc.; (f) Methodology to develop a thesaurus; (g) Pre-Co ordinate and post co-ordinate system and indexing:

PRECIS, POPSI etc. and; (h) Special types of indexing: KWIC, KWOC, Cyclic etc.

Paper 4. Information Technology

To provide the students with a basic knowledge of the application of (a) Computer technology and communication techniques; (b) Reprography and printing technology to information system and services; (c) Information theory, coding etc; (d) Planning and design of information technology application to libraries and information centres.

5.2 *Elective Papers (Group two)*

Group two consists of three papers in each area of L&IS. It aims to provide a thorough study in specific areas of L&IS which can provide substantial knowledge to the problems of specialised area and make available competent professionals (Personnel) in the respective fields. It reveals that each area of study should be specified in its right perspective and plan out the appropriate curriculum to resolve the problem of specialized area.

The area of specialization in L&IS education at MLIS level may be as under:

1. Library classification
2. Library cataloguing
3. Information science
4. Computer application in libraries
5. Library system (any one)
   (a) Public library;
   (b) Academic;
   (c) Research and special;
   (d) Law;
   (e) Medical;
   (e) Agriculture, etc.

5.2.1 *Outlines of Elective Papers*

Each of the specialised area mentioned above consists of three papers each of 100 marks.

The outlines of the above described area of specialisation would be as under:

(1) *Library Classification*

(a) To acquaint students with the advances in the library classification theory;
(b) Library classification practice to acquaint students with the UDC and colon classification of non-conventional and micro documents; and
(c) Research trends in library classification and its evaluation.

(2) *Library Cataloguing*

(a) To acquaint students with the advances in the library cataloguing theory;
(b) Library cataloguing practice to acquaint students with the A.A.C.R. II and classified catalogue code in the cataloguing of periodicals and complex titles; and
(c) Research trends in library cataloguing and its evaluation. By offering classification and cataloguing practice it is aimed to produce the teachers of library and information science.

(3) *Information Science*

(a) Information retrieval;
(b) Information systems and programmes; and
(c) Planning of information service in library.

(4) *Computer Applications*

(a) Computer science;
The details can be drawn out in consultation with computer scientists;
(b) Computer applications in libraries; and
(c) Planning of computer application and its problems.

(5) *Library System*

(i) Public library
- (a) Importance of library in the society
- (b) Library legislation
- (c) Library movement at the global level.

(ii) Academic library
- (a) University library
- (b) College library
- (c) School library

(iii) Research and special library
- (a) Law Library
- (b) Medical library
- (c) Agriculture library

5.3 *Dissertation (Group three)*

The aim should be to develop ability of the student to identify problem areas, apply methods of research and design experiments in finding solutions to the problems; to formulate research proposals; and to effectively present the dissertation on assigned topic.

6. Conclusion

It can be concluded that in the present context the existing MLIS syllabi seem to be out-moded, and much emphasis should be laid on specialisation in library and information science field.

In the context of Open Universities conducting library and information science courses through distant education system it is worth while to go in for specialisation.

17

NEW EDUCATION POLICY AND RESTRUCTURING OF L&IS CURRICULUM IN MARATHWADA UNIVERSITY

A. A. VAISHNAVA

1. Introduction

The role of educational system is to generate new knowledge in all fields within the reach of human mind and develop principles, methodology and guidelines for the application of knowledge for benefiting society, provide knowledge and skills for solving the problem of development. It should enable a student to develop an understanding and perspective of physical and social environment. Therefore, research and development have been accepted as essential ingredients of the educational system.

Education should lay down emphasis on socio-economic well being, competence and creativity of individual, which includes:

(i) Physical, intellectual and aesthetic development of personality;
(ii) Inclusion of scientific temper, democratic, moral and spiritual values;
(iii) Development of self-confidence to innovate and face unfamiliar situations;
(iv) Creation of an awareness of physical, social, technological, economic and cultural development;
(v) Fostering healthy attitude to dignity of labour and hard work;
(vi) A commitment to principles of secularism and social injustice;
(vii) Dedication to uphold the integrity, honour and foster the development of the country; and
(viii) Promotion of international understanding.[1]

India now stands on the threshold of 21st century. The younger educated generation, which is going to enter in the 21st century, should be ready to accept the challenges of the coming century. Hence the Government of India formulated the National Policy on Education in 1986.

The document has given a place of special importance to higher education. It states that "Higher education can prove ideas and men to give shape to future. The quality of life and pace of development of any nation depends on the ideological climate, the widespread perception of history, culture, tradition, values, and the feeling of confidence in human capability. To overcome material, social and spiritual problems of living, higher education supplies a wide range of increasingly sophisticated and overchanging variety of manpower needed in industry, agriculture, administration and services".[2]

2. Factors Forcing Educational Restructuring

(1) There is a widespread concern and a general consensus about the deterioration and irrelevance of educational system. It cannot be improved by marginal changes. The system has to be restructured by fundamental changes in priorities, contents, methodologies of teaching and learning systems etc, which will develop inspiration in the students to be good citizens by transforming social, cultural and economic environment, establish environment for tolerance and cooperation, promote welfare of the poor and the disadvantaged, and augment and modernise production. It is believed that education is the best instrument to achieve these objectives.

(2) India is one of the few countries of the world which has its own satellites in space. It has a large network of television and radio stations. There is considerable manpower capable of developing programmes and telecast them through television network.

(3) Under the computer literacy programmes, computers are being distributed in schools to demystify the computer, and provide children with minimal skills for handling these.

(4) The last but not the least reason for reorientation of educational process is to consider the issues such as delinking of degrees and jobs, linkages between manpower and education, vocationalisation etc.[3]

Considering these factors, a design for an integrated strategy for education has to evolve from national priorities, resource constraints, and the essential interdependence of different programmes.

3. Implementation of the National Policy on Education

In consideration with the suggestions given by National Policy on Education 1986, chapter IV - Higher Education, the Marathwada University appointed a committee consisting of senior academics and administrators. Different study groups were constituted by the committee to consider different aspects of the policy. One of such study groups was set up for restructuring of the courses at undergraduate level.

The study group[4] on restructuring of undergraduate courses pointed out that:

(1) Basically the idea of UGC is to introduce foundation courses to broaden the understanding, particularly of current issues of growth, development, and national integration before the country.

(2) Courses of applied nature were desired to be introduced so that one could get away from the traditional combinations and take into account emerging needs of the society and emerging new disciplines. This was considered to be a positive factor in improving employment opportunities and serving the manpower needs at the same time. Restructuring of courses had particularly become important in view of the introduction of new pattern of education. It was felt that the opportunity be utilized to modernise the courses as well as to enrich the contents and to make them relevant to social needs and aspirations and to respond to emerging needs of trained manpower in different sectors.

The study group by and large accepted the pattern suggestion by UGC, i.e., (1) Foundation course, (2) Core course, and (3) Courses of applied nature.

3.1 *Restructuring and Scheme of Marking*

Restructuring of courses, modification in curriculum and the scheme of marking will be as follows:

(1) The restructuring of undergraduate courses suggested by UGC as well as National Policy on Education emphasizes introduction of common foundation course at the undergraduate level in all faculties. Hence at the first year level of B.A., B.Sc., B.Com., one paper in Foundation Course of 100 marks is proposed to be introduced.

(2) At the I and II year level, in all three faculties, two core (basic course of optional subjects) subjects with two papers each, and one applied (applied to core subjects or of interdisciplinary nature) subject with two papers are proposed. But for the third year of all these courses, since there are no language papers at the third year level, two core and one applied subjects shall have three papers each. This will facilitate extensive study of the concerned subject at the third year level by the student. The respective faculties and Boards of Studies will have to design the structure of core, applied, and interdisciplinary papers.

(3) At the first and second year level the applied papers may be related to the core. However, at the third year two applied papers may be related to core and one may be of interdisciplinary nature.

The following shall be the scheme of courses at B.A. level where practicals are prescribed.

Year	Subject	No. of papers		Marks per Paper		Total for one year	Grand total
		Th	Pr	Th	Pr		
First Year	English	1	—	100	—	100	
	Second language	1	—	100	—	100	
	First core	2	1	100	100	100	
	Second core	2	—	100	—	100	
	Applied	2	—	100	—	100	
	Foundation	1	—	100	—	100	
						1000	1000

Second year	English	1	—	100	—	100	
	Second language	1	—	100	—	100	
	First core	2	1	100	100	300	
	Second core	2	—	100	—	200	
	Applied	2	—	100	—	200	
						900	900
Third year	First core	3	1	100	100	400	
	Second core	3	—	100	—	300	
	Applied	3	—	100	—	300	
						1000	1000
			Grand Total				2000

The Marathwada University has introduced L&IS as optional subject at B.A. I, II & III year level from 1985. The Ad-hoc Board in L&IS has suggested to introduce L&IS as one of the optionals at B.Sc and B.Com level which is under consideration of the Academic Council of the university.

To fit L&IS at the undergraduate level as per the formula, the Adhoc Board in L&IS is likely to suggest the following papers as core and applied subjects respectively.

Year	Subject	No. of papers		Marks
		Theory	Practicals	
First year	*First core*			
	Library administration	1	—	100
	Library classification	1	—	100
	Classification practical	—	1	100
	Second core			
	Library administration	1	—	100
	Library organisation	1		100
	Applied course			
	Philosophy of librarianship	1	—	100
	Library and society	1	—	100
Second year	*First core*			
	Library organisation	1	—	100
	Theory of cataloguing	1	—	100
	Cataloguing practical	—	1	100

	Second core			
	Library classification	1	—	100
	Theory of cataloguing	1	—	100
	Applied course			
	User study	1	—	100
	Technology and libraries	1	—	100
Third year	*First core*			
	Information service	1	—	100
	Resource sharing	1	—	100
	Conservation of library material	1	—	100
	Information service practical	—	1	100
	Second core			
	Information service	1	—	100
	Resource sharing	1	—	100
	Conservation of library material	1	—	100
	Applied course			
	Marketing libraries and information services	1	—	100
	Library management techniques	1	—	100
	Computer and telecommunication technology	1	—	100

4. Factors Responsible for Restructuring of MLIS Curriculum

(1) It is thought that when L&IS is one of the optionals at undergraduate level, then admission to higher courses in library science will be given to those who had chosen one of the core subject and applied subject as Library and Information Science.

(2) Marathwada University has started one-year B Lib Sc course from 1968 and one-year M Lib Sc course from 1985. Instead of B Lib Sc and M Lib Sc course of one year duration, there should be two-year M Lib Sc course as that of Madras University, which will be on par with other M.A., M.Com., or M.Sc., courses.

(3) As per new education policy document, "Effective steps should be taken to see that only those with scholastic aptitude enter in higher education. At the post-graduate level in the formal stream, the need for encouraging only those students who have

good academic record assumes great urgency".[5]

(4) Though the syllabi of B Lib Sc and M Lib Sc courses have been revised from time to time, considering restructuring of undergraduate courses and introduction of L&IS as one of the core and applied subjects at undergraduate level, it is necessary to restructure MLIS curricula on the basis of modified curricula of L&IS subject at undergraduate level.

(5) MLIS is a professional post-graduate course. After passing MLIS course we are recognised as librarians and information scientists. The L&IS profession does not operate in isolation. It is conditioned by the environment within which it exists. Changes in the environment produce the need for the changes in the L&IS profession.

(6) The environment in which L&IS services have to perform is changing significantly. These environmental changes are the results of socio-economic, demographic, political, educational, and technological changes.

(7) Industrialisation, productivity, marketing, emphasis on innovations, products for experts, unemployment, short time working, growing number of retired people, socially disadvantaged and disabled people, emphasis on the use of modern information technology in basic and higher education, developments in computer technology and telecommunication technology, availability of public resources, their distribution to the development of library and information services, its priority, ownership and control of information services, freedom of information, legislation etc are the factors responsible to change the information environment.[6]

(8) As a result of changing information environment, market needs of information specialists are also changing. Advertised posts in India and abroad can be categorised as: on-line searching, introduction of new technology, in house database creation, data presenting, technical services, technological forecasting, index development, market research, business marketing, community development etc. (This categorisation is as per the functions assigned to the information scientists).

(9) The library and information scientists in the changing information environment are required to offer information services regarding authorship, editing, printing, primary publishing, document delivery, collection management consideration,

database, catalogue production, thesaurus construction, system design and management, on-line computing and searching, management of resources, records and archives, information analysis, marketing research, advise, brokerage, signposting and referral, exhibitions, consultancy etc.

(10) The information transfer process requires development of skills of wide range parallel with the library and information skills.

In view of the factors listed above it is necessary to restructure MLIS curricula.

5. Objectives of Two-year MLIS Course

Considering the National Policy on Education, changes in socio-economic, political, educational and technological environment, and changing information environment the objectives of two-year MLIS course should be:

(i) To enable the student to understand and appreciate the functions and purposes of library services in society;
(ii) To give the students an understanding of the basic principles of the theory and practice of library services;
(iii) To train the students in the technique and management of library system;
(iv) Appreciation of the developing role of library and information service agencies in the socio-economic, cultural areas of community life in different countries;
(v) Familiarity with major aspects of information analysis and retrieval;
(vi) Identification of library problems and ability to carry out service programmes; and
(vii) Familiarity with various technologies and their applications to library services etc.

Considering these objectives of two year MLIS course, the curriculum for the course should be:

Year	Subject	No. of papers		Marks
		Theory	Practical	
First year MLIS	Communication and Society	1	–	100
	Library Planning and Management	1	–	100
	Collection development Classification and Indexing	1	–	100
	Information Science and Information Service	1	–	100
	General Theory of Cataloguing	1	–	100
	Classification practical	–	1	100
	Cataloguing practical	–	1	100
	Information Service Practical	–	1	100
			Total	900
Second year MLIS	(A) *Compulsory papers:*			
	International and Comparative librarianship	1	–	100
	Information control and techniques	1	–	100
	Management techniques for Library and Information centres	1	–	100
	(B) *Any one paper from the group*			
	Academic library system	1		100
	Public library system			
	Special library system			
	Research library system			
	(a) (C) *Optional papers (one)*			
	Information science and information service			
	Management of Information centres	1	–	100
	Elements of information science	1	–	100
	Evaluation of information systems	1	–	100
	Information service	1	–	100
	Information service (Pr)	–	1	100

(b) Technology and Libraries	4	1	500
Reprographic and micrographic technology	1	—	100
Computer and Telecommunication technology	1	—	100
Application of computer in library and information work	1	—	100
Software preparation and database management	1	—	100
Practical work on computer	—	1	100
		Total	900

6. Conclusion

The two year MLIS course will not include the paper on research methodology, statistics and the work on dissertation. However, these papers will be included in M. Phil course which is to be introduced in a short course of time.

REFERENCES

1. India, Ministry of Education, Challenge of Education — a policy perspective. New Delhi, Ministry of Education, Government of India, 1986, p 67.
2. *Ibid.* p 6.
3. *Ibid.* pp 69-72.
4. Marathwada University, Committee on Implementation of National Policy on Education (1989): Report, pp 12-23.
5. India, Ministry of Education, *Op cit.*, p 94.
6. Library Association Professional Education and Training for Library and Information work: a review. London, Library and Information Services Council, 1986, pp 2-9.

18

LIBRARY AND INFORMATION SCIENCE EDUCATION IN INDIA : A Literature Analysis

SEWA SINGH

1. Introduction

1.1 *Genesis of Library Literature*

About hundred and ten years ago the first article on library education was written by none other than the father of librarianship, Melvil Dewey on the need for apprenticeship for libraries. It was published in the *Library Journal*[1], the first professional journal in the world. Three years later an article was written by Whitney on the selection and training of library assistants.[2] In all, about eight articles were reportedly published during the 19th century, but their number increased multifold during the present century.

1.2 *Genesis of Library Literature in India*

In India the first article on Library and Information Science (L&IS) education was written in 1930 on the training of librarians.[3] It was followed in 1952 by an article on the "Memoirs of Library Research Circle, Delhi".[4] Further, twc articles were published in 1953 one was produced by the late Dr D.B. Krishna Rao on "Research in Library Science" and the other by S. Parthasarthy on "Training of Library Personnel in India". These two were included in the book *Library Science in India*, edited by K. Chandrasekhran for the Madras Library Association.

1.3 *Environmental Changes*

The last about hundred years of world L&IS education had seen many changes: from simple training/apprenticeship of librarians to library education, to library science education to library and information science education with increased emphasis on information science as a result of the application of the new information technology of computers and computer courses. It has aimed to attempt some structural changes in L&IS courses so as to update them to meet the changing environments in the library and information centres.

2. **Purpose**

This paper attempts to serve two broad purposes.

2.1 *Analysis*

The main objective is to make an analysis of literature on L&IS education published in India and abroad by Indian authors. The literature included for analysis is produced not only by L&IS teachers, librarians, and other researchers, but also by some foreign authors as well as computer experts or information technologists who contributed to both Indian and foreign sources in the form of articles, reports, lectures, etc.

2.2 *Bibliographical Control*

On making a survey of literature it was discovered that so far no single comprehensive bibliography is available on L&IS Education in India. The bibliography compiled by the Indian National Scientific Documentation Centre[5] covers only the period of 1955-1966, hence incomplete. Another bibliography, though global in scope and coverage, lacks completeness in respect of Indian literature.[6]

3. **Parameters**

3.1 *Sources*

3.1.1 *Journals*

The rate of growth of L&IS journals has been fairly good during the last fifty years or so. From the *Modern Librarian* of the 1930 to the *Indian Journal of Information, Library and Society* of the late 1980s, there are about 25 L&IS journals being currently published in India in English language. Though some other journals are being published in some of the regional languages, the choice for this paper is restricted to English language journals only.

3.1.2 *Foreign Journals*

Some foreign journals were also scanned, particularly those where the Indian authors have a tendency to publish their contributions.

3.1.2 *Bibliographies*

Three bibliographies of Indian library literature covering the period from 1950 to 1985 are thoroughly scanned[7-9] to collect data on L&IS Education. These bibliographies attempt to provide a reasonably comprehensive overview of literature on the subject.

3.1.4 *Edited Books, etc*

Articles on L&IS Education included in some edited books are also covered. Various seminar/conference papers on L&IS Education published in monograph form or made available in mimeographed form have also been included in this study.

The world famous *Encyclopaedia of Library and Information Science,* edited by Allen Kent, et al. was also scanned to cull out one article on the theme of this paper.

In this way every sincere effort has been made to carefully scan all the possible sources up to the year 1989. However, there still may be a possibility of some of them eluding this investigator due to a variety of reasons. A comprehensive coverage to that extent is, therefore, not claimed though that has been the cherished desire.

4. Bases of Analysis

After thoroughly scrutinising all the sources as mentioned above, entries on cards were prepared and subsequently grouped under the following broad subject headings which indeed are the conceptual concepts:

(1) L&IS Education, in general
(2) Library Schools
(3) L&IS Curricula and Courses
(4) Methods of Teaching
(5) Continuing Education
(6) Institutes and Workshops
(7) Research in L&IS Education

All the contributions included in this study on the abovementioned subjects/conceptual divisions have carefully been analysed. The analysis reveals the following:

(1) Chronological Scatter
(2) Subject/Conceptual Scatter
(3) Article Scatter
(4) Geographical Scatter
(5) Author Scatter

5. Chronological Scatter

A total of 674 contributions have been recorded on L&IS Education up to the end of 1989. A chronological distribution of these articles is given in the Table 18.1.

It is evident from the data presented in Table 18.1 that the range of minimum contributions is between 1 and 123: one article has been published each in 1952, 1956 and 1961; while in 1987 as many as 123 articles etc. have been published in various sources.

The average number of contributions for all these years works out at about 17.7 articles per annum. The contributions for the years 1965 to 1968, 1972,1978, 1982 and 1984 is higher than the yearly average, while for the remaining years it is lower.

There has been a general increase in the contributions by scholars to L&IS Education since the mid-eighties, and it has been further pushed up during the last decade since 1976 and still further during the eighties. For a still better view, this information is condensed as in Table 18.2.

TABLE 18.1: Chronological Distribution

Year	No. of Articles	Percentage	Year	No. of Articles	Percentage
1952	1	0.15	1971	8	1.18
1953	2	0.29	1972	28	4.15
1954	4	0.59	1973	8	1.18
1955	2	0.29	1974	14	2.07
1956	1	0.15	1975	6	0.89
1957	2	0.29	1976	14	2.07
1958	5	0.74	1977	16	2.37
1959	5	0.74	1978	39	5.78
1960	3	0.44	1979	16	2.37
1961	1	0.15	1980	15	2.22
1962	7	1.03	1981	34	5.04
1963	5	0.74	1982	25	3.71
1964	2	0.29	1983	16	2.37
1965	21	3.11	1984	21	3.11
1966	19	2.82	1985	23	3.41
1967	26	3.85	1986	45	6.67
1968	18	2.67	1987	123	18.24
1969	6	0.89	1988	45	6.67
1970	11	1.63	1989	38	5.63
			Total	674	100.00

TABLE 18.2: Cumulative Chronological Distribution

Years	No. of Articles	10-years Cumulations	%5-years	%10-years
1951-55	9		1.33	
1956-60	16	25	2.37	3.70
1961-65	36		5.34	
1966-70	80	116	11.87	17.21
1971-75	64		9.49	
1976-80	100	164	14.83	24.32
1981-85	119		17.65	
1986-89	251	370	37.24	54.89
Total	674		100.00	

It is clear from Table 18.2 that the decades of 1960s, 1970s and 1980s comprise the highest number of articles, i.e, 17.21 per cent during the 1960s, while it is 24.32 per cent during the 1970s, and 54.89 per cent during the 1980s. But the contribution during the 1980s is more than double that of the 1970s and still more than the combined contributions of the 1960s and the 1970s. Even during the last four years of the 1980s (i.e., 1986-89), the contributions of the scholars are as much as 251 which is higher than any other decade. This is due to the celebration of the Centenary Year of L&IS Education in 1987 all over the world, and also the 75th year in India.

The general increase (excepting 1987) in contributions may be attributed to growth in L&IS Education in general during this period. There has also been growth in the number of L&IS schools, increase in the strength of the faculty, rise in the number of working librarians all over the country. To assert this fact the growth in the LIS schools at the university level and the initiation of new LIS Journals is parallely compared with the growth of literature in the following Table 18.3:

TABLE 18.3: Growth of Literature Compared with Growth of Courses and Journals

Period	No. of Articles	No. of University Departments	Cumulated Numbers	No. of Journals	Cumulated Number
Upto 1960	25	14	14	5	5
1961-65	36	11	25	5	10
1966-70	80	07	32	3	13
1971-75	64	12	44	4	17
1976-80	100	04	48	3	20
1981-85	119	20	68	6	26
1985-89	251	04	72	2	28

Table 18.3 reveals that while 18 new teaching departments were opened during the 1960s, 16 of them were established during the 1970s, which means that 50 per cent of the courses were started within these two decades. On the other hand, about 41.5 per cent literature on L&IS education was also published during the same period. Similarly, 15 new L&IS journals were also instituted during the same two decades. However, the total number of articles has gone up during 1981-89, and this increase is also comparable with the setting up of 24 new L&IS schools which is one-third of the total number of the total L&IS journals being published in India in English language. However, literature published during 1980s is more than half of departments in

the country. Similarly, 8 new L&IS journals have also been started during this decade which is also about one-third of the total contributions reported in the professional journals this far.

6. Subject Scatter

The entire field of L&IS Education is divided in components of seven logical subjects, mainly based on the classification divisions of the DDC 20. The total contributions are distributed among these subject divisions. To facilitate the analysis, a combined chronological and subject scatter has also been attempted. Table 18.4 presents the distribution of literature under the subjects identified earlier.

TABLE 18.4 : Subject Scatter

Sr. No.	Subjects	No. of Articles	% of Total	Ranking
1.	L&IS Education, in general	374	55.48	1
2.	L&IS Schools	23	3.41	6
3.	L&IS Curricula	134	19.88	2
4.	Methods of Teaching	40	5.93	4
5.	Continuing Education	36	5.34	5
6.	Institutes/Workshops	16	2.37	7
7.	Research in L&IS Education	51	7.56	3

The data presented in the above table reveals that more than 55 per cent of the total contributions have been made in the area of L&IS Education in general alone including its origin and development in India and other countries. The second largest contribution, though much behind, is on syllabus and curriculum of L&IS Education, the quantitative output of which stands at 134 articles (i.e., 19.88%) only. The neglected areas are L&IS Schools and Institutes, coupled with Methods of Teaching and Continuing Education/Professional development.

A combined distribution of chronological and subject scatter as presented in Table 18.5 gives a better picture.

The combined analysis of chronological and subject scatter makes amply clear that the decades of 1970s and 1980s were the most productive. If we analyse it on the basis of 5-year data as presented in Table 18.5 above it comes to the notice that there is consistent growth in the total contributions with the exception of 1971-75 block when it dwindles down to 64 articles from 80 for 1966-70. However, during 1976-80 there is steep rise to 100 contributions from the earlier figure of 64.

TABLE 18.5 : Chronological and Subject Scatter

Periods	L&IS Education	L&IS Curriculum	L&IS Schools	Methods of teaching	Continuing education	Institutes/ workshops	Research	Total
1951-55	6	—	—	1	—	—	2	9
1956 60	11	—	2	—	—	—	2	15
1961-65	29	6	—	—	—	—	1	36
1966-70	51	11	4	7	—	—	7	80
1971-75	39	14	2	7	—	2	—	64
1976-80	74	8	3	5	—	2	8	100
1981-85	67	22	3	4	15	—	8	119
1986-89	97	73	9	16	21	12	23	251
Total	374	134	23	40	36	16	51	674

The sharp increase during the block years 1986-89 is because 1987 was celebrated as the Centenary Year of L&IS Education all over the world and 75th year in India. During 1987 at least two seminars were organised which brought out two volumes of papers adding about 80 contributions.

7. Author Scatter

If we have an evaluative look at the author scatter particularly from the point of view of team research, it can be safely concluded from the data presented in Table 18.6 below that the maximum articles have been published by the single authors, hence team research is not popular among the Indian authors in Library and Information Science (L&IS), while according to Dr de Solla Price it is quite common in sciences.

8. Geographical Scatter

In the present study it is estimated that 70 contributions out of the total of 674 are from the foreign-based authors in this area. Most of them are from such countries like Great Britain, U.S.A., Germany, Australia, Nigeria, etc. They have published in India, L&IS journals as well as in some books edited for various purposes by Indian authors.

TABLE 18.6 : Author Scatter

Periods	Single Authors	Two Authors	Three and more Authors	Corporate Authors	Title
1951-55	8	—	—	—	—
1956-60	16	—	—	1	—
1961-65	33	1	—	3	1
1966-70	62	8	1	4	5
1971-75	50	9	1	2	3
1976-80	70	10	—	—	3
1981-85	63	12	1	1	4
1986-89	180	46	8	2	15

From among the Indian authors most of them are based at Delhi, Bangalore, Calcutta, Madras, Lucknow, Nagpur, Jaipur, Varanasi, Waltair, Hyderabad, Amritsar, Ujjain, Chandigarh, Pune, Patiala, Mysore, Bombay, Trivandrum, etc. In view of this, there seems to be need for more contributions to the existing body of professional literature in the area of L&IS Education by the professionals from places other than those mentioned above. It will provide a more representative character to the body of professional literature and will give a real Indian look.

9. **Article Scatter**

All the 674 contributions included in the present study have not appeared in the periodical literature alone; they have also been reported in and culled from the edited books from time to time as mentioned earlier. In the Table 18.7 below is presented the journalwise distribution of articles.

Twenty-eight Indian and two foreign journals have published 419 articles which work out about 62.16 per cent of the total contributions on L&IS Education during the last about 40 years or so. In the two foreign L&IS journals only two articles by Indian authors are published on the theme of the study.

TABLE 18.7: Article Scatter

Sr. No.	Name of Journal	No. of Articles	Ranking
Indian			
1.	ALIS Bulletin	09	13
2.	Annals of ILA (ceased)	01	18
3.	Annals of Library Science and Documentation	17	10
4.	CLIS Observer	05	14
5.	College Librarian	01	18
6.	DRTC Annual Seminar	26	06
7.	Herald of Library Science	69	01
8.	IASLIC Bulletin	25	07
9.	ILA Bulletin	27	05
10.	Indian Journal of Information, Library and Society	02	17
11.	Indian Journal of Library Science	01	18
12.	Indian Librarian (ceased)	34	03
13.	International Information, Communication and Education	19	09
14.	International Librarian (ceased)	02	17
15.	International Library Movement	21	08
16.	Journal of Library and Information Science	15	11
17.	LIBRA	15	11
18.	Library & Librarian (ceased)	02	17
19.	Library Herald	29	04
20.	Library Progress (International)	09	13
21.	Library Science Annual	01	18
22.	Library Science with a Slant to Documentation and Information Studies	37	02
23.	Library Today	01	18
24.	Lucknow Librarian	26	06
25.	MLAI Bulletin	01	18
26.	National Librarian (ceased)	13	12
27.	RILISAR Bulletin	03	16
28.	University News	04	15
Foreign			
1.	International Classification	01	18
2.	Unesco Bulletin for Libraries (ceased)	01	18
	Total	419	

The remaining 255 contributions are taken from books edited for various purposes, seminar volumes, etc, including one article which is taken from the *Encyclopaedia of Library and Information Science.*

As reported in Table 18.7, the maximum articles (69) have been published in the *Herald of Library Science*, edited by Prof P.N. Kaula from Lucknow. It is followed by *Library Science with a Slant to Documentation* from DRTC with 37 articles to its credit. It has, since 1987, introduced slight change in its title by suffixing "and Information Studies". *Indian Librarian,* which was the oldest Indian L&IS journal till it ceased publication in 1982, occupies the third place with 34 articles on L&IS Education. Next in order of contributions on this theme is the *Library Herald* of the Delhi Library Association. Six of the Indian professional journals have published only one article each on the theme of the study thus far.

9.1 *Contribution in Book Form*

The literature produced in book form (27 books) during the 80-years history of L&IS Education in India is not adequate. Among these are two bibliographies (referred to in Section 12) which are not complete in their coverage in one respect or the other. Two books are produced on the Methods of Teaching, another two on L&IS Schools, and one on Research in Library and Information Science. Some books are published as a result of some seminars organised by various institutions.

This literature in book form is published during the last 30 years only: and no book on the subject of study has been brought out during the 1950s or earlier.

9.2 *Seminars*

According to an estimate about 28 national and state level seminars have been held on L&IS Education, again most of them during the three decades of 1960s, 1970s and 1980s, and the most recently held Seminar is the one organised by the Indian Association of Teachers in Library & Information Science (IATLIS) as its Seventh Seminar during 14-16 December, 1989 at the Saurashtra University, Rajkot on the theme of 'Restructuring of L&IS Curriculum'.[10] But the papers presented at these Seminars/conferences have not been brought out in published form in almost all the cases. However, the papers and the proceedings must be published for the sake of wider circulation and permanent use and record.

9.3 *Dissertations*

It is estimated that about 21 Master's dissertations have been written on various aspects of L&IS Education by the M.L.I.Sc students in partial fulfilment of the requirement of this Degree.

It is reported that a couple of Ph.D. theses have been completed by scholars on manpower development combining educational aspects, and that work on few more Ph.D. theses is in progress in different areas of L&IS Education.

9.4 *Conclusions and Suggestions*

(i) From the analysis given above, it is amply clear that literature on L&IS Education in India started sprouting in early 1950s and has been proliferating since 1960s. It went up from 25 contributions (for 1951-60) to 116 (for 1961-70) to 164 (for 1971-80). It further went up to 370 (for 1981-89) at an annual growth rate of about 41 articles for the eighties.

(ii) There is so far no specialised periodical devoted exclusively to L&IS Education in India. In the light of the above analysis indicating proliferation in literature, there is need for such a specialised journal.

(iii) Since 1965 no special report has been prepared on the state of the art or the existing situation of L&IS Education in India. There is now need for such documents also.

(iv) In view of the growth of literature during the last 40 years or so there is probably need for some kind of change or diversification in the course contents for the present as well as the future. This is particularly desirable when the new technology in the form of computers is round the corner. It is therefore imperative that the 'think tanks' of the profession invest more thought and wisdom in the writings on computer application to libraries and library education so as to bring the L&IS Education in India technologically well advanced.

(v) There has been mushroom growth in recent years of new courses at various levels, particularly at the Certificate/Diploma level. There is pressing need to contain such a trend as it has some negative effect on university education in particular and the profession of librarianship in general.

(vi) There is need to evaluate the L&IS Education in India by the

University Grant Commission, as it did in 1965. A critical appraisal of such issues as admission requirements, curriculum and syllabi, standards, accreditation, methods of teaching, research needs, comparative studies, teaching, faculty, National Policy of L&IS Education, etc.

(vii) It is suggested that concrete steps must be taken by the individuals, agencies like the UGC, etc to implement the recommendations of various seminars held so far and thereby give a new look to the structure of L&IS Education in India enabling it to meet the manpower needs, information needs of the 21st century.

REFERENCES

1. Melvil Dewey, "Apprenticeship of librarians", *Library Journal*, 4, May 1879, p.147.
2. James Lyman Whitney, "Selection and training of library assistants", *Library Journal*, 7, 1882.
3. "Training of librarians", *Modern Librarian*, Nov. 1930.
4. S. Parthasarthy, "Memoirs of library research circle, Delhi", *Annals of Indian Library Association*, 2, 1953.
5. Indian National Scientific Documentation Centre, New Delhi, *Bibliography for Librarianship, 1955-66*, New Delhi: INSDOC, 1967 (mimeographed).
6. I.V. Malhan and Shabad Kapoor, *Library Education: An Annotated Bibliography*, New Delhi : Metropolitan, 1982.
7. R.G. Prasher, *Indian Library Literature: An Annotated Bibliography*, New Delhi: Today and Tomorrow's, 1971.
8. Sewa Singh and I.V. Malhan, *Indian Library Literature: An Annotated Bibliographic Guide, 1971-80*, New Delhi : Today and Tomorrow's, 1986.
9. Sewa Singh, *Indian Library Literature, 1981-85: An Annotated Bibliographic Guide*, New Delhi : Ess Ess Publications, 1988.
10. *Iatlis Communication*, 10 (1) Jan. 1990.

INDEX

CICIL LIST

CONCEPTS IN COMMUNICATION, INFORMATICS & LIBRARIANSHIP

(CICIL)

General Editor: **S.P. AGRAWAL**

CICIL-1 Development of Library Services in India: Social Science Information
S.P. Agrawal Rs. 150

CICIL-2 Development of Documentation in India: Social Science Information
S.P. Agrawal Rs. 250

CICIL-3 UNESCO and Social Sciences: Retrospect and Prospect
S.P. Agrawal and **J.C. Aggarwal** Rs. 250

CICIL-4 INDIANA : A Bibliography of Bibliographical Sources
M.K. Jain Rs. 200

CICIL-5 Dimensions of Library and Information Science: Kaula Festschrift
V. Venkatappaiah (Eds.) Rs. 600

CICIL-6 Book Numbers: Some Indian Methods
M.P. Satija and **S.P. Agrawal** Rs. 100

CICIL-7 National Policy for University Libraries in India: Problems and Perspectives
N.B. Inamdar and **L.S. Ramaiah** (Ed.) Rs. 250

CICIL-8 Media Utilisation for the Development of Women and Children
B.S. Thakur and **Binod C. Agrawal** Rs. 150

CICIL-9 Terrorism: An Annotated Bibliography
Susheela Bhan (Ed.) Rs. 275

CICIL-10 Transnational Library Relations: The Indo-American Experience
M.B. Konnur Rs. 175

CICIL-11 Geography of Marketing and Commercial Activities in India (Documentation on Research Information)
R.S. Dixit Rs. 130

CICIL-12 Information India 1988: Global View
S.P. Agrawal and **J.C. Aggarwal** Rs. 200

CICIL-13 Women's Education in India: Historical Review, Present Status and Perspective Plan
S.P. Agrawal and **J.C. Aggarwal** Rs. 360

CICIL-14 Cultural Communication in India: Role and Impact of Phonograms
J.M. Ojha Rs. 220

CICIL-15 Second Historical Survey of Educational Development in India: Select Documents 1985-1989
S.P. Agrawal and **J.C. Aggarwal** Rs. 490

CICIL-16 Documentation Encyclopaedia of UNESCO and Education
J.C. Aggarwal and **S.P. Agrawal** Rs. 800 (set of 2 parts)

CICIL-17 Attitude Towards Information: A Study of Post-Graduate Teachers and Researchers in Social Sciences
N.G. Satish (in press)

CICIL-18 Librarianship and Bureaucratic Organisation: A Study in the Sociology of Library Profession in India
P.K. Jayaswal Rs. 175

CICIL-19 Literature Search
K.A. Isaac Rs. 150

CICIL-20 Child Education in India: Index to Scholarly Writings in Indian Educational Journals and Newspapers since independence
S.P. Agrawal and **Naresh Kanta** Rs. 100

CICIL-21 Lok Sabha and Vidhan Sabha Elections in India 1989 & 1990: Process and Results with Comparative Study of Manifestos
S.P. Agrawal and **J.C. Aggarwal** Rs. 250

CICIL-22 Islamic Studies in India: A Survey of Human, Institutional and Documentary Sources
Mohamed Taher Rs. 180

CICIL-23 Panchayati Raj: An Annotated Bibliography
N.B. Inamdar, N.G. Satish and **Anil Takalkar** 290

CICIL-24 Information India 1989-90: Global View
S.P. Agrawal and **J.C. Aggarwal** Rs. 500

CICIL-25 First Handbook of Psychological and Social Instruments
Udai Pareek and **T. Venkateswara Rao** Rs. 500

CICIL-26 Educational and Social Uplift of Backward Classes: At What Cost and How? Mandal Commission and After
S.P. Agrawal and **J.C. Aggarwal** Rs. 275

CICIL-27 Mass Media and New Horizons: Impact of TV & Video an Urban Milieu
H.R. Trivedi Rs. 180

CICIL-28 Indian Writings on Education : An Indicator to Indian Educational Journals Grouped by Subject Deseriptors 1979 to 1986 (in two parts)
S.P. Agarwal Rs. 900 (per set)

CICIL-29 Nation in Crisis
S.P. Agrawal and **J.C. Aggarwal** Rs. 200

CICIL-30 Information India 1990-91: Global View
S.P. Agrawal and **J.C. Aggarwal** Rs. 500

CICIL-31 Development of University Libraries in India after Independence **O.P. Gupta** Rs. 270

CICIL-32 Handbook on Child : With Historical Background
Pramila Pandit Barooah Rs. 320

CICIL-33 Weaker Section in Indian Society : Undiscovered Past, Uncertain Present and Unpredictable Future : Index to Writings in Indian Scholarly Journals and 10 National Newspapers Classified under 1500 Descriptors 1886-1990
S.P. Agrawal and **Rajeev Kumar Sharma** Rs. 600

CICIL-34 Communication Informatics and Librarianship in India : An Introductory Guide to Publications Based on a Survey of Libraries in Capital City of India
S.P. Agrawal and **Pushpa Rani Sharma** Rs. 720

CICIL-35 Problems of Collection Development in Special Libraries
M.S. Sridhar Rs. 225

CICIL-36 National Information Resources for Social Sciences in India : Mobilisation, Dispersal and International Enhancement
S.P. Agrawal Rs. 225

CICIL-37 Modern History of Punjab : A Look Back into Ancient Peaceful Punjab Focusing Confrontation and Failures Leading to Present Punjab Problem, and a Peep Ahead : Relevant Select Documents
J.C. Aggarwal and **S.P. Agrawal** Rs. 400

CICIL-38 India Information Sources : Economics and Business
Kyllikki Ruokonen and **Manohar Lal** Rs.

CICIL-39 Educational Planning in India : With a Slant to Educational Financing and Administration, Vol. 1, Reports of Committees and Commissions, Five Year Plans, Statistical Tables
J.C. Aggarwal and **S.P. Agrawal** Rs. 650

CICIL-40 Integrated Library System : Two Case Studies : Latin America and India
Maria Luiza Rigo Pasquarelli, Rosaly Favero Krzyanowski, Ines Maria M. Imperatriz and S.P. Agrawal Rs. 160

CICIL-41 Social Science Information in India: Effort towards Bibliographical Control
S.D. Vyas Rs. 300

CICIL-42 Higher Education in India Since Independence: U.G.C. and Its Approach
O.P. Gupta Rs. 360

CICIL-43 Government and Politics in India: A Bibliographical Study of Contemporary Scenario Chronicling Rajiv Gandhi Era
S.P. Agrawal and **Rajeev Kumar Sharma** Rs. 500

CICIL-44 Second Handbook of Psychological and Social Instruments
D.M. Pestonjee Rs. 300

CICIL-45 Development/Digression Diary of India; 3D Companion Volume to Information India: 1990-91
S.P. Agrawal Rs. 200

CICIL-46 Development/Digression Diary of India; 3D Companion Volume to Information India: 1991-92
S.P. Agrawal Rs. 300

CICIL-47 Information India 1991-92: Global View
S.P. Agrawal and **J.C. Aggarwal** Rs. 500

CICIL-48 Committees and Commissions in India 1974, A Concept's Project, Compiled by a team of professionals guided by **Virender Kumar** (Vol. 12) Rs. 450

CICIL-49 Committees and Commissions in India 1975, A Concept's Project, Compiled by a team of professionals guided by **Virender Kumar** (Vol. 13) Rs. 450

CICIL-50 Committees and Commissions in India 1976, A Concept's Project, Compiled by a team of professionals guided **Virender Kumar** (Vol. 14) Rs. 450

CICIL-51 Committees and Commissions in India 1977, A Concept's Project, Compiled by a team of professionals guided by **Virender Kumar** (Vol. 15) (in four parts) Rs. 450 each

CICIL-52 Committees and Commissions in India 1978, A Concept's Project, Compiled by a team of professionals guided by **Virender Kumar** (Vol. 16) (in two parts) Rs. 450 each

CICIL-53 Subject Guide to Communication, Informatics and Librarianship in India (Based on a Survey of Library Holdings in Capital City of India)
S.P. Agrawal and **Pushpa Rani Sharma** Rs. 400

CICIL-54 Restructurring of Library and Information Science Curriculum
A. Tejomurty Rs. 250